INTERNATIONAL TRADE THEORY
AND
REGIONAL INCOME DIFFERENCES

UNITED STATES 1880–1950

CONTRIBUTIONS
TO
ECONOMIC ANALYSIS

70

Honorary Editor

J. TINBERGEN

Editors

J. JOHNSTON

D. W. JORGENSON

J. WAELBROECK

NORTH-HOLLAND PUBLISHING COMPANY

AMSTERDAM · LONDON

INTERNATIONAL TRADE THEORY AND REGIONAL INCOME DIFFERENCES

UNITED STATES 1880–1950

by

ERLING OLSEN

University of Copenhagen

1971

NORTH-HOLLAND PUBLISHING COMPANY

AMSTERDAM · LONDON

Library of Congress Catalog Card Number: 77–140487
ISBN: 0 7204 3170 0

Publishers:

NORTH-HOLLAND PUBLISHING COMPANY — AMSTERDAM
NORTH-HOLLAND PUBLISHING COMPANY, LTD. — LONDON

Denne afhandling er af det rets- og statsvidenskabelige fakultet ved Københavns universitet antaget til offentlig at forsvares for den statsvidenskabelige doktorgrad.

København,   SVEN DANØ
14. juli 1970   Prodekan

PRINTED IN THE NETHERLANDS

Introduction to the series

This series consists of a number of hitherto unpublished studies, which are introduced by the editors in the belief that they represent fresh contributions to economic science.

The term *economic analysis* as used in the title of the series has been adopted because it covers both the activities of the theoretical economist and the research worker.

Although the analytical methods used by the various contributors are not the same, they are nevertheless conditioned by the common origin of their studies, namely theoretical problems encountered in practical research. Since for this reason, business cycle research and national accounting, research work on behalf of economic policy, and problems of planning are the main sources of the subjects dealt with, they necessarily determine the manner of approach adopted by the authors. Their methods tend to be 'practical' in the sense of not being too far remote from application to actual economic conditions. In addition they are quantitative rather than qualitative.

It is the hope of the editors that the publication of these studies will help to stimulate the exchange of scientific information and to reinforce international cooperation in the field of economics.

THE EDITORS

Preface

The idea behind this book began to take shape when Carl Iversen and Richard W. Downar gave me an opportunity to visit America as an International Fellow of the American Council of Learned Societies 1962–1963. I spent the Fall semester at the Regional Science Department, University of Pennsylvania, where I took courses given by i.a. Walter Isard and William Warntz. The Winter and Spring semesters were spent at the Department of Economics, University of Chicago. Harry G. Johnson, Zvi Griliches and Theodore W. Schultz gave me inspiration and advice. So did Edward L. Ullman and Morgan D. Thomas of the Department of Geography, University of Washington, Seattle, where I spent the Summer semester 1963.

When I returned to my teaching obligations in Copenhagen I had little time to work on the book and the work did in fact stop when I was elected to the Parliament in 1964.

In 1966 I took a leave from Parliament to go to Stockholm, Sweden, joining the staff of the Institute for International Economic Studies. Gunnar Myrdal, Ingvar Svennilsson, Karin Kock, Östen Johansson, Gunnar Adler-Karlsson, Nils Lundgren, Per Wijkman, Egon Matzner and Tarlok Singh took part in our afternoon teas from which I profited very much. Being in Stockholm also meant being indebted to Lars Matthiessen, Staffan Burenstam Linder, Peter B. Kenen, Erik Lundberg and Ernst Söderlund.

Having finished the theoretical part of the book in 1967, I returned to Denmark where the rest of the book was written. Karl Vind, Axel Mossin and Poul Nørregaard Rasmussen were most helpful at this stage of the work.

The Danish State General Science Foundation and the Danish State Social Science Research Council financed the computations done by Bjarne Andersson at the Northern Europe University Computing Centre, Kongens Lyngby, Denmark, and at the Atomic Energy Commission Research Establishment, Risø, Denmark. K. Søe Højberg and Christian Suusgaard were of great help.

The manuscript was edited by Connie Wall to whom I am most grateful. Caroline Burton read the proofs and did a very good job. Secretarial assistance was generously given to me by Gunvor Åberg and Gunilla Forsmann in Stockholm and by Else Haugebo, Grete Stenør and Gerda Suenson in Copenhagen.

The University of Pennsylvania Press and the Regional Science Research Institute in Philadelphia, Pennsylvania, kindly gave me permission to reproduce material from two books by William Warntz.

Copenhagen,   ERLING OLSEN
September 1970

Introduction

1 Teaching international trade theory has given me both pleasure and pain.

Pleasure, because I like to give simple answers to simple questions. And international trade theory seemed to me to be the last branch of economics where this could be done. When students asked why nations trade I could answer: "Due to differences in relative factor endowments . . ." When they asked which commodities a country would export I could answer: "Those whose production demands a relatively great input of its relatively abundant factor . . ." And when they asked how international trade would affect the remuneration of the factors of production I could answer that Heckscher and Ohlin had proved that free international trade under the usual and well-known assumptions would lead to an equalization of factor prices.

But I felt it more and more difficult to believe in what I was telling these students. Teaching has therefore given me an increasing amount of pain. The international discussion around the Leontief paradox created serious doubts about the relevance of the Heckscher–Ohlin theory of why nations trade and which goods they export. Also the empirical studies of the regional income differences in the United States made me doubtful about the relevance of the factor-price equilization theorem. After all, the world seemed to be much more complicated than the Hechscher–Ohlin theory assumed.

2 Some economists tried to get out of this dilemma by giving up simplicity. They emphasized that Ohlin's 1933 book[1] left

[1]Bertil Ohlin, *Interregional and international trade*, Harvard Economic Studies, vol. 39, Harvard University Press, Cambridge, Mass. 1933.

many doors open and started elaborating and refining the Heckscher–Ohlin model. They developed new analytical tools. They wrote books and articles which were fascinating from an intellectual point of view. But they did not add much to our knowledge of interregional and international trade.

Others threw away most of the Heckscher–Ohlin theory trying to create something entirely different. Staffan Burenstam Linder[2] emphasized demand where Heckscher and Ohlin had emphasized supply. Members of the school of Social Physics[3] used analogies from physics in their analyses of social phenomena and Gunnar Myrdal[4] substituted his principle of circular or cumulative causation for the principle of stable equilibrium. The new approaches were very promising. Their basic ideas turned our attention to aspects of interregional and international trade which had hitherto been regarded as less important. But when the new models were elaborated and refined, they added little – if anything – to our knowledge of interregional and international trade.

This gave me the impression that little could be achieved by further elaborations and refinements. But it might be fruitful to integrate the basic ideas of the different theories. That is what I shall try to do.

3 I want to integrate the basic ideas of the different theories into a model determining the regional income differences within a nation. I then want to compare the results of the theoretical analysis with an empirical material to see whether the model makes sense at all.

4 Part 1 of the book surveys the theories whose basic ideas shall be integrated. Like most textbooks it organizes the material

[2]Staffan Burenstam Linder, *An essay on trade and transformation*, Almqvist & Wiksell, Uppsala 1961.
[3]See e.g. John Q. Stewart, "Demographic gravitation: evidence and application", *Sociometry*, vol. 11, no. 1–2, February-May 1948, pp. 31–58.
[4]Gunnar Myrdal, *Economic theory and underdeveloped regions*, Duckworth & Co., London 1957.

by asking the two fundamental questions: "Why do nations trade?" (chapter 1) and "How does trade affect the international distribution of income?" (chapter 2).

Part 2 presents (in chapter 3) an economic model in time and space focussing regional income differences. This part is the main contribution of the book.

Part 3 evaluates the model on the basis of available data from the United States 1880–1950. For many, very good reasons it was not possible to do an ordinary econometric analysis. So, all that is done is a very preliminary evaluation of whether the model makes sense. Chapter 4 tells about the method to be used. Chapter 5 presents the data to be used. Chapter 6 describes how the data are used tentatively to produce some very rough, preliminary estimates of the parameters of the model. In the following chapters these estimates are used running the model under different assumptions. Chapter 10 brings the conclusions.

Appendix A shows the sensitivity of the model to a change in the value of one of the parameters.

Appendix B presents the computer programmes used. They have been written by Mr. Bjarne Anderson, Institute of Statistics, University of Copenhagen.

Appendix C is a post scriptum telling about a sensitivity analysis on a hybrid computer. The computer's display screen was filmed and the film is sold as an extra to this book.

Contents

Contents

List of symbols

a Number of inhabitants per member of the labour force.

d_{ij} Distance between region i and region j ($i = 1, 2, \ldots, n$; $j = 1, 2, \ldots, n$).

e The base of natural logarithms.

E_i^t Average number of years of school completed by the labour force at time t in region i ($i = 1, 2, \ldots, n$).

E^t Average number of years of school completed by the labour force at time t in the nation.

K_i^t Stock of capital at time t in region i ($i = 1, 2, \ldots, n$).

K^t Stock of capital at time t in the nation.

L_i^t Stock of labour (labour force) at time t in region i, or flow of labour services per unit of time from time t to time $t + 1$ in region i ($i = 1, 2, \ldots, n$).

Lt Stock of labour (labour force) at time t in the nation, or flow of labour services per unit of time from time t to time $t + 1$ in the nation.

n Number of regions.

P_i^t Stock of inhabitants (population) at time t in region i ($i = 1, 2, \ldots, n$).

P^t Stock of inhabitants (population) at time t in the nation.

r_i^t Flow of return on capital from time t to time $t + 1$ in region i per unit of capital employed at time t in region i ($i = 1, 2, \ldots, n$).

r^t Flow of return on capital from time t to time $t + 1$ in the nation per unit of capital employed at time t in the nation.

R Marginal rate of substitution between capital and labour.

U_i^t Percentage of the population at time t in region i ($i = 1, 2,$

..., n) living in urban communities with more than a given number of inhabitants.

U^t Percentage of the population at time t in the nation living in urban communities with more than a given number of inhabitants.

$_iV^t$ Gross economic population potential at time t in region i ($i = 1, 2, \ldots, n$).

V^t Average of the nation's n regional gross economic population potentials at time t.

w_i^t Flow of wage payments from time t to time $t+1$ in region i per member of the labour force at time t in region i ($i = 1, 2, \ldots, n$).

w^t Flow of wage payments from time t to time $t+1$ in the nation per member of the labour force at time t in the nation.

y_i^t Flow of regional income from time t to time $t+1$ in region i per inhabitant at time t in region i ($i = 1, 2, \ldots, n$).

y^t Flow of national income from time t to time $t+1$ per inhabitant at time t in the nation.

Y_i^t Flow of regional income from time t to time $t+1$ in region i ($i = 1, 2, \ldots, n$).

Y^t Flow of national income from time t to time $t+1$.

β_i^t Substitution parameter from time t to time $t+1$ in the aggregate CES production function of region i ($i = 1, 2, \ldots, n$).

β^t Substitution parameter from time t to time $t+1$ in the aggregate CES production function of the nation.

γ_i^t Efficiency parameter from time t to time $t+1$ in the aggregate CES production function of region i ($i = 1, 2, \ldots, n$).

γ^t Efficiency parameter from time t to time $t+1$ in the aggregate CES production function of the nation.

Γ Rate of growth per unit of time in the nations capital stock.

δ_i^t Distribution parameter from time t to time $t+1$ in the aggregate CES production function of region i ($i = 1, 2, \ldots, n$).

δ^t Distribution parameter from time t to time $t+1$ in the aggregate CES production function of the nation.

ζ Income-per-capita elasticity of capital.

η Rate-of-return elasticity of capital.

ϑ Gross-economic-population-potential elasticity of capital.

Θ Natural rate of growth per unit of time in the nation's labour force.

H Income-per-capita elasticity of labour.

κ Income-per-capita elasticity of efficiency.

λ Wage elasticity of labour.

Λ Rate of growth per unit of time in the efficiency parameter in the CES production function of the nation.

μ Gross-economic-population-potential elasticity of labour.

ν Education elasticity of efficiency.

Ξ Rate of growth per unit of time in the average number of years of school completed by the labour force of the nation.

π Urbanization elasticity of efficiency.

σ Elasticity of substitution between capital and labour.

τ Gross-economic-population-potential elasticity of efficiency.

υ Income-per-capita elasticity of education.

φ Urbanization elasticity of education.

χ Gross-economic-population-potential elasticity of education.

ψ Income-per-capita elasticity of urbanization.

ω Gross-economic-population-potential elasticity of urbanization.

Ω Rate of growth per unit of time in the nation's level of urbanization.

PART 1

International trade theory

CHAPTER 1

Why do nations trade?

1   This fundamental question has been answered in three different ways:

The Heckscher–Ohlin school has explained international trade by national differences in relative factor endowments.[1]

Staffan Burenstam Linder has emphasized similarities in preferences and in income.[2]

Economists, sociologists and geographers working with so-called gravity models have explained trade as a function of population, income and distance.[3]

In the following, we shall present the assumptions, the main reasoning and the conclusions of each of the three groups of theories.

The Heckscher–Ohlin school

2   The Heckscher–Ohlin theory has been presented in many, and often very sophisticated, versions.[4] Here, it shall be

---

[1] See Eli F. Heckscher, "The effect of foreign trade on the distribution of income", *Ekonomisk Tidskrift*, vol. 21, 1919, pp. 497–512 (in Swedish) and *Readings in the theory of international trade*, Blakiston, Philadelphia 1949, pp. 272–300. See also Bertil Ohlin, *Interregional and international trade*, Harvard Economic Studies, vol. 39, Cambridge, Mass. 1933.

[2] See Staffan Burenstam Linder, *An essay on trade and transformation*, Almqvist & Wiksell, Uppsala 1961.

[3] See i.a. H. Linnemann, *An econometric study of international trade flows*, Contributions to Economic Analysis, vol. 42, North-Holland Publ. Co., Amsterdam 1966.

[4] See e.g. Murray C. Kemp, *The pure theory of international trade*, Prentice Hall, Englewood Cliffs, New Jersey 1964 and J. L. Ford, *The Ohlin–Heckscher theory of the basis and effects of commodity trade*, Asia Publishing House, monograph no. 6, London 1965.

shown in a two-country, two-commodity, two-factor model illustrated by the Savosnick edition of the Edgeworth box diagram.[5]

It is assumed that two countries, I and II, are producing two commodities, X and Y, with two factors of production, capital (K) and labour (L).

In each country capital and labour are available in fixed quantities. There is perfect competition in both the markets for commodities and the markets for the factors of production. Commodities can move freely between nations (no barriers to trade, no transportation costs), whereas capital and labour are assumed to be internationally immobile.

It is further assumed that production functions are identical in the two countries, that the marginal rate of substitution between factors is increasing in the production of both commodities, and that there are constant returns to scale, i.e., that production functions are linear and homogeneous. Finally, it is assumed that the production of X is capital-intensive while the production of Y is labour-intensive.

3   The increasing marginal rate of substitution between factors means that if the production of a commodity shall remain unchanged, it is necessary to substitute an increasing amount of capital for every unit of labour withdrawn from the production of the given commodity, and vice versa. Isoquants will therefore be convex to the origin as shown in fig. 1.1.

The constant returns to scale mean, that if the input of both capital and labour in the production of a commodity is multiplied by the constant κ, then the output of the commodity will also be multiplied by κ. The production functions can therefore be represented by only one isoquant for each commodity. All other isoquants can be constructed by "blowing up" or "shrinking down" the representative isoquants.

[5]See Kurt M. Savosnick: "The box diagram and the production possibility curve", *Ekonomisk Tidskrift*, November 1958, pp. 183–197.

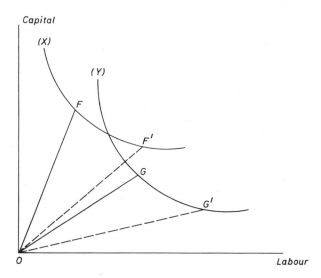

Fig. 1.1. Isoquants for the capital-intensive commodity *X* and the labour-
intensive commodity *Y*.

That the production of *X* is capital-intensive while the production of *Y* is labour-intensive means that at any given common
factor price ratio, the ratio of capital to labour must be greater
in the production of *X* than in the production of *Y*. In fig. 1.1
one ratio between factor prices is expressed by the slope of the
tangents to the isoquants through the points F and G respectively. Another ratio between factor prices is illustrated by the
tangents through F′ and G′. The corresponding capital to labour
ratios are expressed by the slopes of OF, OG, OF′ and OG′.

4   Fig. 1.2 shows the Savosnick edition of the Edgeworth–
Bowley box diagram.
   The side O_xP of the box represents a country's labour endowment, while the side O_yP represents its capital endowment.
   O_x is the origin of the *X*-isoquant map and O_y is the origin of
the *Y*-isoquant map. The solid line O_xQO_y is the so-called contract curve. It is the locus of all points where an *X*-isoquant

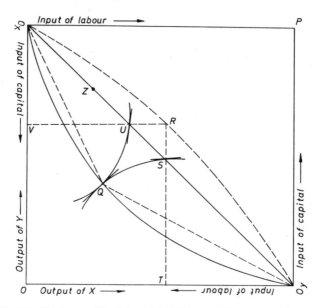

Fig. 1.2. The Savosnick edition of the Edgeworth-Bowley box diagram.

and a *Y*-isoquant have a common tangent. The contract curve indicates all the efficient allocations of the factors of production and it must be located below the diagonal $O_x O_y$. This is because the production of *X* is more capital-intensive than the production of *Y*. The capital-labour ratio in the production of *X* is expressed by the slope of the straight line from the relevant point on the contract curve, e.g., the point Q to O_x whereas the capital–labour ratio in the production of *Y* is expressed by the slope of the straight line from the same point on the contract curve to O_y. From any point on the contract curve the straight line to O_x must therefore be steeper than the straight line to O_y, and this will only be the case if the contract curve lies below the diagonal $O_x O_y$.

5 The diagonal itself is most interesting because it is assumed that production functions are linear and homogeneous. In this case any ray through the origin of an isoquant map has two

important properties. First, the marginal rate of substitution between the factors of production is the same along the ray. This means, e.g., that the tangents to the X-isoquants have the same slope in all the points of the ray O_xO_y through the origin O_x of the X-isoquant map. The tangents to the Y-isoquants will also have the same slope along the diagonal. Fig. 1.2 shows, however, that the slope of the tangents to the Y-isoquant will be greater than the slope of the tangents to the X-isoquant along the diagonal.

Secondly, when production functions are linear and homogeneous any ray through the origin of an isoquant map can be used to measure production quantitatively. If the isoquant through the point S on the diagonal represents, say, a production of 20 units of the commodity X we know that an X-isoquant through the point Z halfway between O_x and S will represent 10 units of X, etc.

As shown by Savosnick it is now possible to measure the output of X along the side OO_y of the box diagram. This can be done by a vertical projection of the points of the diagonal upon OO_y. Using the same technique the output of Y can be measured quantitatively along OO_x.

6 We can now construct the production possibility curve, also called the transformation curve, corresponding to the contract curve of fig. 1.2.

The X-isoquant through point Q on the contract curve intersects the diagonal at point S. This point is projected vertically into point T upon the X-axis of the XY map in fig. 1.2. In the same way we move from point Q via point U to point V upon the Y-axis. We now have the coordinates of the point R on the transformation curve corresponding to the point Q on the contract curve. The other points of the transformation curve are constructed by the same method.

7 We now want to show how differences in a nation's relative factor endowments influence the shape of its transformation curve. To facilitate the comparisons we assume that the nation under any circumstances will have a total factor endowment making it possible to produce a given amount of the commodity X, and that the changes in its relative factor endowments only will be of importance for its production of the commodity Y.

The box diagram OO_xPO_y in fig. 1.3 corresponds to the box diagram in fig. 1.2. The curve O'_yO_y is the X-isoquant representing the amount of X produced when all the resources of the country are devoted to the production of this commodity. The curve O_xA is the Y-isoquant representing the amount of Y produced when all the resources of the country are used in the production of Y.

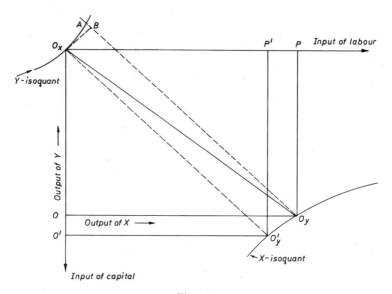

Fig. 1.3.

We now illustrate a change in the relative factor endowments of the country by moving the origin of the Y-isoquant map to the left along the X-isoquant through O_y. Fig. 1.3 shows a marginal change in the factor endowments. The origin of the Y-isoquant map has been moved from O_y to O'_y. The ratio of capital to labour has increased since the supply of capital has been increased (by OO') while the supply of labour has been diminished (by PP').

The new factor endowment illustrated by the box $O'O_xP'O'_y$ makes it possible to produce the same maximum amount of X as the old factor endowment did because O'_y is a point on the X-isoquant through O_y. But how great will the new maximum production of Y be?

To answer this question we shall draw a line O_yBA parallel to the diagonal in the new box diagram and a line O_xB parallel to the tangent to the X-isoquant through O_y. Because the change in the relative factor endowment is assumed to be marginal we can approximate the part $O_yO'_y$ of the X-isoquant with the tangent through O_y. Therefore $O_yO'_yO_xB$ is a parallelo-gram and the point B indicates in the old Savosnick box dia-gram the maximum input of capital and labour in the production of Y after the change in the country's factor endowment. The point B falls short of the point A because the slope of the Y-isoquant at O_x is greater than the slope of the X-isoquant at O_y which is parallel to O_xB. Therefore, if the maximum production of X remains unchanged and the country's overall capital–labour ratio is increased, then the maximum production of Y will be decreased.

8   In fig. 1.4 it is shown by the same method that the maximum production of Y is increased if the maximum production of X is unchanged and the country's overall capital–labour ratio is decreased. The change in the relative factor endowment is assumed to be a marginal one, whereby the amount of capital is reduced with OO'' and the amount of labor increased with PP''.

Summarizing, it can be said that if the maximum production of the capital-intensive commodity X remains unchanged and the country's relative factor endowment is changed, the maxi-mum production of the labour-intensive commodity Y will decrease if labour becomes relatively more scarce and increase if labour becomes relatively more abundant.

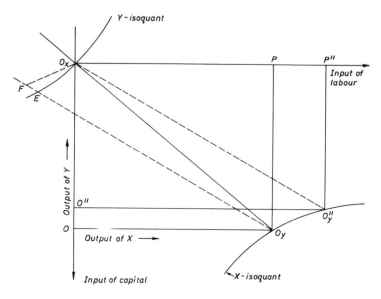

Fig. 1.4.

9 Fig. 1.5 shows five different shapes of a country's transformation curve. Of these, LM corresponds to the transformation curve of fig. 1.2, while the other transformation curves are constructed by the technique illustrated in figs. 1.3 and 1.4.

10 We now assume that two countries, I and II, have identical preferences for the commodities X and Y and that these preferences can be illustrated by a given community indifference map. The indifference curves of this map are supposed to have the same properties as individual indifference curves. In fig. 1.6 the convex curve through R_I and R_{II} is an arbitrary community indifference curve from the given community indifference map.

It is further assumed that the countries have different relative factor endowments. In country I, capital is relatively abundant and the transformation curve has the shape indicated by LM′ in fig. 1.5. In country II labour is relatively abundant and the transformation curve has the shape indicated by LM″ in fig. 1.5.

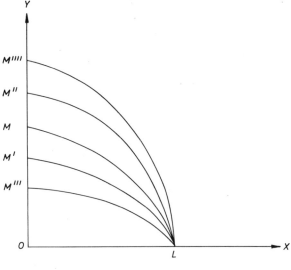

Fig. 1.5.

Tangent to the community indifference curve in fig. 1.6 we now draw two transformation curves: one the same shape as LM′ in fig. 1.5 illustrating the relative factor endowment of country I, and one the same shape as LM″ illustrating the relative factor endowment of country II.

Fig. 1.6 shows that the common slope of the indifference curve and the transformation curve is smaller in R_I than in R_{II}. This implies that the relative price of the capital-intensive good, X, is lowest in country I where capital is relatively abundant, whereas the relative price of the labour-intensive good, Y, is lowest in country II where labour is relatively abundant.

If there are no costs for transportation, no tariffs and no other barriers to trade, the capital-rich country I will export the capital-intensive commodity X and import the labour-intensive commodity Y. Corresponding to this, the labour-rich country II will export the labour-intensive commodity Y and import the capital-intensive commodity X.

This is, in short, the Heckscher–Ohlin theory of why nations trade.

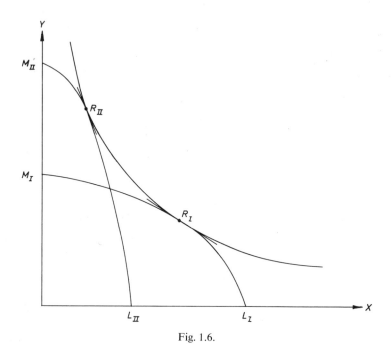

Fig. 1.6.

Staffan Burenstam Linder

11 A different answer to the question has been given by
Staffen Burenstam Linder who only accepts differences in
relative factor endowments as an explanation of trade in
primary products. International trade in manufactures must,
according to Linder, be explained by similarities in internal
demand and differences in industrial tradition.[6]

Linder's theory of international trade is different from
Heckscher's and Ohlin's because his assumptions are different.
Heckscher and Ohlin assume constant returns to scale but
Linder finds economies of scale important. If a country shall be
an efficient producer of a given commodity, it must produce

[6]See Staffan Burenstam Linder, *op. cit.*, pp. 87–91.

this commodity on a large scale. In a world of imperfect know-ledge, entrepreneurs will be more aware of profit opportunities arising from domestic needs than of those arising from needs abroad. Therefore it is more likely that large-scale production is started in countries with a great internal demand for the commodity in question.

When such production has been taken up the producers will develop and accumulate technical know-how, making production even more efficient. Linder therefore assumes that countries with a tradition in the production of an industrial commodity may be more efficient producers than other countries.

From this follows, firstly, that a nation may be an exporter of an industrial commodity if it has a great internal demand for this commodity and a tradition for producing it on a large scale. Secondly, that the commodity is likely to be imported by countries which also have a great internal demand for this product but no tradition for producing it on a large scale.

The internal demand for a product is to a great extent determined by a country's per capita income and by the population's individual preferences. Therefore, Linder concludes that nations trade in industrial products because of similarities in income and preferences.

The Social Physics school

12   The third group of answers to the question of why nations trade has been given by the members of the so-called Social Physics school. Most of these scientists are not economists and their approach to economic problems is different from the conventional one.

The term social physics was made familiar to social scientists by the Princeton astronomer, John Q. Stewart,[7] who found it

[7]See John Q. Stewart: "Suggested principles of 'social physics'," *Science*, vol. 106, (N.S.), 1947, pp. 179–180 and John Q. Stewart: "Concerning social physics", *Scientific American*, vol. 178, 1948, pp. 20–23.

rewarding to regard the members of a social group as the individual molecules of a physical mass and to analyse the interaction between social groups in the same way as the physicists analyse interaction between masses.

Stewart defined three demographic concepts analogous to the physical concepts, gravitational force, gravitational energy and gravitational potential. Around these concepts he constructed the so-called gravity and potential models for the analysis of social phenomena.[8]

In the following, we shall first describe the basic gravity and potential models developed by Stewart and other members of the school of Social Physics. Secondly, we shall see how these models have been used to explain interregional and international trade.

13 Let us assume that a metropolitan region has a total population P. The region is divided into n subareas, and there are no significant differences among subareas in preferences, income, age distribution, occupational structures, etc., of their population. The population of subarea i is P_i and there are P_j inhabitants in subarea j. The distance between i and j is d_{ij}.

Stewart's concept, demographic force, follows the formula of gravitational force as a constant times the product of the two masses divided by the square of the distance separating them.

We can therefore express the demographic force, F, created by the subareas i and j of the metropolis by

$$F = G \frac{P_i P_j}{(d_{ij})^2},$$

(1.1)

where G is a constant.

The demographic energy, E, corresponding to gravitational energy can be expressed by

$$E = G \frac{P_i P_j}{d_{ij}}.$$

(1.2)

[8]See John Q. Stewart: "Demographic gravitation: evidence and application", *Sociometry*, vol. 11, no. 1–2, February–May 1948, pp. 31–58.

Stewart's third concept, demographic potential, corresponding to gravitational potential, is defined by eqs. (1.3) and (1.4).

$$_iV_j = G\,\frac{P_j}{d_{ij}}\,. \tag{1.3}$$

Eq. (1.3) determines the demographic potential $_iV_j$ produced at point (subarea) i by the mass (population) at j.

The total demographic potential at i produced by all the relevant masses (subareas) is designated $_iV$ and determined by

$$_iV = G\,\sum_{j=1}^{n}\frac{P_j}{d_{ij}}\,. \tag{1.4}$$

Stewart developed his gravity and potential models on the basis of eqs. (1.1) and (1.4) respectively and he found it important to use as many analogies from physics as possible in his studies of social interaction.

14   Stewart was, however, not the first scientist to use analogies from physics in the analysis of social phenomena, and his pupils were not convinced about the importance of using exactly the same models as the physicists.

As early as the middle of the nineteenth century H. C. Carey observed the presence of gravitational force in social phenomena[9] and W. J. Reilly presented his model of retail trade gravitation in 1929[10]. But the take-off in social physics did not come until the 1940's with the works of Stewart and the Harvard sociologist, George K. Zipf.[11] An excellent survey of the

[9]See H. C. Carey, *Principles of social science*, J. B. Lippincott & Co., Philadelphia 1858–59.

[10]See William J. Reilly, "Methods for study of retail relationships", *University of Texas Bulletin*, no. 2944, November 1929.

[11]See George K. Zipf: "The P_1P_2/D hypothesis on the intercity movement of persons", *American Sociological Review*, vol. 11, December 1946, pp. 677–686, and George K. Zipf, *Human behavior and the principle of least effort*, Addison-Wesley Press, Reading, Mass. 1949.

literature on gravity, potential and spatial interaction models has been written by Walter Isard and David F. Bramhall.[12]

This survey tells about the more or less successful use of gravity and potential models in the analysis of interaction between spatially separated social groups, e.g., the exchange of letters, the number of telephone calls, the passenger traffic by railway between cities, the migration of labour, etc. The survey also tells us how the members of the school of Social Physics came farther and farther away from the analogies to physics.

15 In their presentation of the basic gravity and potential models, Isard and Bramhall adopt a rather simple probability point of view.[13]

They assume that the total number of internal trips in our metropolis is T during a given period. The number of trips taken by a representative individual is therefore $K = T/P$ during the period in question.[14]

If transportation neither took time nor cost money, we could expect a representative individual living in subarea i to use P_j/P of his K internal trips to go to subarea j. And since subarea i has P_i inhabitants, we should expect the number of trips T_{ij} originating in subarea i and terminating[14] in subarea j to be

$$T_{ij} = K \frac{P_i P_j}{P}.$$ (1.5)

16 We know, however, that our assumptions are unrealistic. Travelling does take time and costs money. We can therefore

[12]Published as chapter 11 in Walter Isard, *Methods of regional analysis*, M.I.T. Press and Wiley, New York and London 1960, pp. 493–568.

[13]Isard and Bramhall say in a footnote that in developing this point of view, they draw heavily upon J. D. Caroll and H. W. Bevis, "Predicting local travel in urban regions", *Papers and Proceedings of the Regional Science Association*, vol. 3, 1957.

[14]The K internal travels are all supposed to be return-trips. A trip originating in subarea i and terminating in subarea j is a return-trip from i to j.

speak of a friction of distance and Isard and Bramhall would like to measure this friction.

They now assume that we have the data on the actual number of personal trips between each pair of subareas. The actual number of trips originating in subarea i and terminating in subarea j is designated I_{ij}. For each pair of subareas they plot the ratio I_{ij}/T_{ij} of actual to expected trips and the distance d_{ij} on a graph with logarithmic scales.[15]

Finally, Isard and Bramhall assume that they get a picture like fig. 1.7.

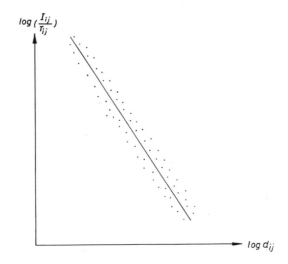

Fig. 1.7. Relation between distance and the ratio of actual to expected person trips (hypothetical data).

If this is the case, they can fit a straight line to the plotted data. The equation of this line is

$$\log \frac{I_{ij}}{T_{ij}} = a - b \log d_{ij}. \tag{1.6}$$

The constant a is defined by the intercept of the straight line

[15]Like Isard and Bramhall we shall here ignore a discussion of the interaction of a subarea with itself.

with the Y-axis and the constant b is defined by the slope of the straight line.

If c is the antilog of a, we have

$$\frac{I_{ij}}{T_{ij}} = \frac{c}{(d_{ij})^b}$$

or

$$I_{ij} = \frac{cT_{ij}}{(d_{ij})^b}. \tag{1.7}$$

From this equation we derive the basic gravity model of Isard and Bramhall by substituting the right-hand side of eq. (1.5) for T_{ij} and by letting the constant $G = cK/P$.

$$I_{ij} = G \frac{P_i P_j}{(d_{ij})^b}. \tag{1.8}$$

17 The basic gravity model was developed in the analysis of the number of personal trips from subarea i to subarea j of the metropolitan region. And the basic potential model can be derived in an analysis of the number of trips from subarea i to all the other subareas.

By addition of $I_{i1} + I_{i2} + \cdots + I_{in}$ we get

$$\sum_{j=1}^{n} I_{ij} = G \sum_{j=1}^{n} \frac{P_i P_j}{(d_{ij})^b}$$

or

$$\frac{\sum_{j=1}^{n} I_{ij}}{P_i} = G \sum_{j=1}^{n} \frac{P_j}{(d_{ij})^b}. \tag{1.9}$$

The left-hand side of eq. (1.9) is the per capita (per unit of mass) interaction of subarea i with all other subareas including itself.[15] This is the potential at i usually designated $_iV$. We can therefore rewrite eq. (1.9) as

$$_iV = G \sum_{j=1}^{n} \frac{P_j}{(d_{ij})^b}.$$ (1.10)

Eq. (1.10) is the basic potential model of Isard and Bramhall.

18 Two things are important in Isard's and Bramhall's presentation of gravity and potential models.

First, that the models are developed from a probability point of view without assuming that the interaction between social groups follows the laws of interaction between physical masses.

Secondly, that the whole presentation stands and falls with fig. 1.7. Here it is assumed that we get a good functional relationship between the ratio of actual to expected trips (I_{ij}/T_{ij}) and distance (d_{ij}).

This is, in fact, the crucial point. The gravity and potential models are of value to Isard and Bramhall not because they believe in analogies from physics, but because a number of empirical studies of the friction of distance have proved the usefulness of organizing the data in gravity and potential models.

The difference in the approach between Stewart on the one hand, and Isard and Bramhall on the other, can be seen by comparing the gravity models of eqs. (1.1) and (1.8). To Stewart it was important to develop a social physics. He therefore insisted that the exponent to d_{ij} should be 2. But to Isard and Bramhall it was more essential to get a good fit, so they would let the exponent to d_{ij} depend upon the slope of the regression line in their scatter diagram.

19 It may, however, not be enough to vary the exponent to d_{ij} to get good fits. Depending upon the specific problems to be investigated and data available, it may prove useful to apply weights to masses. In a study of trade between regions it might, for example, be appropriate to weigh populations with per capita incomes. It may also prove useful to raise mass to another power than unity or to measure distance in another unit than physical distance.

The general formula of the gravity model should therefore be

$$I_{ij} = G \; \frac{w_i(P_i)^{\alpha}w_j(P_j)^{\beta}}{(d_{ij})^b}. \tag{1.11}$$

Stewart's gravity model is a special case of (1.11) where $w_i = w_j = \alpha = \beta = 1$ and $b = 2$.

Correspondingly, the general formula of the potential model should be

$$_iV = G \sum_{j=1}^{n} \frac{w_j(P_j)^{\beta}}{(d_{ij})^b}. \tag{1.12}$$

Stewart's potential model is a special case of (1.12) where $w_j = \beta = b = 1$.

20 We shall now turn to the use of gravity and potential models in the explanation of interregional and international trade. Here, two major contributions have been made: one by a group of Finnish economists around Penti Pöyhönen, and another by a group of Dutch economists around Jan Tinbergen. Independently of each other the two groups developed very similar gravity models, and they both estimated the parameters of their models in econometric studies.

21 The first Pöyhönen study was received by the editors of Weltwirtschaftliches Archiv on the 3rd of November, 1961. It had to queue up behind other articles accepted by the editors and could not be published until 1963.[16]

---

[16]See Pentti Pöyhönen, "A tentative model for the volume of trade between countries", *Weltwirtschafliches Archiv*, Band 90, Heft 1, 1963, pp. 93–100.

Pöyhönen's gravity model is characterized by three special features:

First, the concept of mass is not population but national income.[17]

Secondly, the concept of distance is not physical distance but cost of transportation.

Thirdly, two new parameters are introduced: an export parameter for the country of export and an import parameter for the country of import.

In terms of the symbols used above, Pöyhönen's gravity model was of the form

$$I_{ij} = GG_iG_j \frac{((Y_i/P_i)P_i)^{\alpha}((Y_j/P_j)P_j)^{\beta}}{(1+hd_{ij})^b}, \tag{1.13}$$

where I_{ij} = the value of the exports from country i to country j,

G_i = the export parameter of country i,
G_j = the import parameter of country j,
Y_i = the national income of country i,
Y_j = the national income of country j,
h = the transportation cost coefficient per unit of distance.

Pöyhönen estimated the parameters of his gravity model in a study of the trade between ten European countries[18] in 1958. He got his data from the statistical publications of the United Nations, and he ended up with an encouraging 0.94 coefficient of multiple correlation.

22 Pöyhönen therefore decided to do a follow-up. Together with Kyösti Pulliainen and Stig-Erik Bergström he formed a research team to do a more ambitious study of world trade.

[17]It could be said that population is weighed by income per capita.
[18]Belgium, Denmark, Finland, Western Germany, Italy, The Netherlands, Norway, Portugal, Sweden and the United Kingdom. Pöyhönen wanted to include the most important European countries in his analysis, but he also wanted to obtain a certain similarity in the modes of transportation. This led him to strive for a predominance of sea transportation, and therefore he had to exclude countries such as France, Switzerland and Austria.

Pöyhönen had studied international trade in 1958. The team was to study the thirteen successive years from 1948 to 1960.

Pöyhönen had studied the trade between ten European countries. The team was to study the trade between sixty-two non-communist countries from all parts of the world.

Finally, Pöyhönen had only estimated the parameters of one gravity model. The team was to estimate the parameters of two alternative models.

Some preliminary results of the team's research were published in 1963.[19]

23 The results showed that the pattern of the commodity flows between the sixty-two countries remained practically unchanged during the period under review. The estimates of the parameters for the various years did not differ significantly from one another.

The new study therefore took away some of the doubts about the results of Pöyhönen's tentative analysis of 1958 data.

24 The extension of the analysis from ten to sixty-two countries also proved reasonably successful. The coefficients of multiple correlation varied between 0.80 and 0.87 which the team found not very high in itself. Taking into account that the sixty-two countries from all over the globe made an extremely heterogeneous group, the coefficients of multiple correlation were, however, found to be of a tolerable order of magnitude.

25 The Finnish research team estimated the parameters of two alternative gravity models. The first one was

$$I_{ij} = G G_i G_j \frac{((Y_i/P_i)P_i)^\alpha ((Y_j/P_j)P_j)^\beta}{(d_{ij})^b}, \qquad (1.14)$$

[19]In the Finnish *Ekonomiska Samfundets Tidsskrift*, Tredje serien, årgang 16, 1963, no. 2. See Pentti Pöyhönen, "Toward a general theory of international trade", pp. 69–77; Kyösti Pulliainen, "A world trade study: an econometric model of the pattern of the commodity flows in international trade 1948–1960", pp. 78–91, and Stig-Erik Bergström, "Den internationella varuhandeln: En teoretisk studie", pp. 92–110.

or the gravity model of eq. (1.13) with the only exception
that physical distance had replaced the cost of transportation
function in the denominator. The cost of transportation function
of (1.13) made the model non-linear and highly expensive to
estimate in a sixty-two-country study. This was the only reason
why it was given up.

26 The alternative model presented by the Finnish research
team included two additional explanatory variables:

First, the concept of market area was introduced. The sixty-
two countries were divided into eight market areas,[20] and it was
assumed that the trade between two countries was influenced by
the size of the market areas to which they belonged. The
larger the market area, the larger the exchange of goods. The
size of a market area I consisting of m countries was measured
by the sum Y_I of the gross domestic products of the countries
belonging to the area

$$Y_I = \sum_{i=1}^{m} Y_i; \quad i \in I. \tag{1.15}$$

Secondly, it was assumed that trade was influenced by geographical location and meteorological conditions. For each
country these circumstances were characterized by the long-
range mean temperature $C°$. It was assumed that the larger the
differences between mean temperatures, the larger the need to
exchange commodities.

The formula of the alternative gravity model thus becomes

$$I_{ij} = GG_iG_j \frac{((Y_i/P_i)P_i)^\alpha ((Y_j/P_j)P_j)^\beta}{(d_{ij})^b}$$

$$\times (Y_I)^\gamma (Y_J)^\delta (1 + |C_i° - C_j°|)^\epsilon, \tag{1.16}$$

where country i belongs to market area I and country j to
market area J. γ, δ and ϵ are parameters.

[20]U.S.A., Canada, Central America, South America, Europe, The Middle East,
Africa and the Far East.

The econometric study showed, however, that the explanatory power of the gravity model was only slightly increased when the size of the market areas and the differences in temperature were taken into account.

27   The first Dutch study of international trade flows was published in 1962 as an appendix to Jan Tinbergen's book *Shaping the world economy*.[21]

The purpose of Tinbergen's analysis was to measure the effects of discrimination in international trade. The actual import and export figures should, for each country, be compared with the trade which could be expected in the absence of discriminating impediments to international trade.

Tinbergen assumed that these impediments were of a stochastic nature. He could therefore determine the standard pattern of international trade in the absence of discrimination by an econometric analysis of the actual trade figures. But first he had to formulate a model.

28   In fact, Tinbergen tried three gravity models: His basic model was in terms of the symbols used here

$$I_{ij} = G \, \frac{((Y_i/P_i)P_i)^\alpha \, ((Y_j/P_j)P_j)^\beta}{(d_{ij})^b}. \tag{1.17}$$

This very simple model was, however, extended into

$$I_{ij} = G \, \frac{((Y_i/P_i)P_i)^\alpha \, ((Y_j/P_j)P_j)^\beta}{(d_{ij})^b} \, (N)^\gamma \, (PR_C)^\delta \, (PR_B)^\epsilon, \tag{1.18}$$

where N = dummy variable for neighbouring countries,
   PR_C = dummy variable for Commonwealth preference,
   PR_B = dummy variable for Benelux preference.

[21]Jan Tinbergen, *Shaping the world economy*, Twentieth Century Fund, New York 1962. Appendix VI: "An analysis of world trade flows", pp. 262–293.

The dummy variable for neighbouring countries was introduced because it was found likely that adjacent countries had more intense trade contacts than the short distance between them could explain. The dummy variables for the Commonwealth and the Benelux preferences were introduced to take account of the political element in the trade of countries belonging to a preferential area.

The third model of the Tinbergen study was

$$I_{ij} = G \frac{((Y_i/P_i)P_i)^\alpha ((Y_j/P_j)P_j)^\beta}{(d_{ij})^b} (G_i)^\gamma, \tag{1.19}$$

where G_i is the so-called Gini coefficient of country i's export commodity concentration. The Gini index is 100 for a country exporting only one commodity, and the more diversified the country's export package becomes, the lower is the value of the index. The Gini coefficient was included in the gravity model because it was supposed that the trade flows of a country that specialized in exporting a small number of products might well differ in size from those of a country with a more diversified export structure.

29 The parameters of eqs. (1.17) and (1.18) were estimated first in an analysis of the trade between eighteen countries[22] in 1958. The results were found encouraging. The analysis was therefore extended to forty-two countries covering about 70 percent of world exports in 1959 and the parameters of models (1.17) and (1.18) were estimated on the 1959 data.

Model (1.19) was used in a study of the trade in 1959 between 28 of the above-mentioned 42 countries.

The coefficient of multiple correlation was only slightly increased when model (1.18) or (1.19) replaced the basic gravity model (1.17) and the average value of the correlation coefficient was not very high, around 0.81.

[22]Brazil, Venezuela, S. Africa, Japan, Canada, U.S.A., Austria, BLEU, Denmark, France, Western Germany, Italy, The Netherlands, Norway, Sweden, Switzerland, UK and Australia.

To Tinbergen it was, however, not unsatisfactory because he expected the actual pattern of trade to deviate substantially from the "ideal" or "theoretical" pattern. After all, these deviations were what he had hoped to identify in his book.

30 The study published by Tinbergen was part of a larger study of world trade flows undertaken by a research team at the Netherlands Economic Institute. In 1966 another member of the team, Hans Linnemann, published an important book.[23]

Linnemann's approach was similar to that of Tinbergen. His basic gravity model

$$I_{ij} = G \frac{(Y_i)^\alpha (Y_j)^\beta}{(P_i)^\gamma (P_j)^\delta (d_{ij})^b} (PR)^\epsilon \qquad (1.20)$$

was a little more complicated. His empirical analysis included the trade of 80 non-communist countries in 1958/60, or about double as many countries as Tinbergen had included in his analysis. His statistical methods of estimation were more sophisticated than those of Tinbergen and, despite the difficulties created by the increase in the number of countries, Linnemann got coefficients of multiple correlation of the same order of magnitude as Tinbergen did.

Linnemann's main contribution is, however, that he, to a higher degree than his predecessors, based his analysis upon an economic theory. He saw no justification at all for the analogies with physical gravitation and he wanted to give an economic explanation of international trade flows.

31 According to Linnemann, nations trade because their domestic patterns of production cannot be expected to coincide with their domestic patterns of demand. Different countries have developed comparative advantages in different fields of production and this makes international trade profitable.

[23]Hans Linnemann, *An econometric study of international trade flows*, Contributions to Economic Analysis, vol. 42, North-Holland Publ. Co., Amsterdam 1966.

Heckscher and Ohlin were of the same opinion but they explained comparative advantages by differences in factor endowments. Linnemann does not.

He believes that comparative advantages are mainly determined by (i) economies of scale and (ii) national differences in technology.

The differences in technical know-how are i.a. explained by time-lags in the geographical diffusion of innovations and Linnemann emphasizes how technical change both creates and destroys comparative advantages. Quoting Romney Robinson[24] and Kindleberger,[25] he further mentions that international trade in itself changes the relative factor proportions within the trading countries. He therefore concludes: "Comparative advantages are predominantly man-made, and their existence is a consequence as much as a cause of foreign trade".[26]

Linnemann does not deny that climate and natural resources have an influence on the pattern of world trade. But he says that this influence should not be overestimated. A theory of international trade should be built up around the man-made comparative advantages and those created by climate and natural resources should be considered as exceptions.

32   The theory, supported by Linnemann, tells us that the trade between two countries is a function of the potential export supply of the exporting country, the potential import demand of the importing country and the resistance to trade between the two countries concerned.

Disregarding the problems of international capital movements, balance of payments surpluses and deficits and differences between national product and national income, a country's

---

[24]Romney Robinson, "Factor proportions and comparative advantage", *Quarterly Journal of Economics*, vol. 70, 1956, pp. 169–192 (part I) and pp. 346–363 (part II). Quotations from p. 346 and p. 361.

[25]Charles P. Kindleberger, *Economic development*, McGraw-Hill, New York 1958. Quotations from p. 243.

[26]Hans Linnemann, *op. cit.*, p. 22.

potential foreign trade can be defined as the gross national product times the potential foreign trade ratio. We may then ask: What determines the potential foreign trade ratio, i.e., the ratio between a country's potential foreign trade and its gross national product?

Linnemann's answer is that there is a strong tendency for the potential foreign trade ratio to vary only in relation to differences in population size between countries.

33 This answer is based upon two assumptions: (i) the existence of economies of scale and (ii) the diversification of demand at higher levels of income.

Comparing two countries with equal per capita incomes but different population size, Linnemann concludes that the larger country will reach or surpass the minimum market size for efficient domestic production in more lines of production than the smaller country does. This should give a negative correlation between the size of population and the foreign trade ratio of a country when we compare countries with equal per capita income.

The interesting thing is, however, that we would have found exactly the same correlation if we had compared countries with different per capita incomes. For, according to Linnemann, there is no reason to believe that a country's foreign trade ratio should vary with its per capita income.

If a country with a given population gets an increase in per capita income, two things will happen. First, the additional demand may for certain commodities bring the home market up to the minimum size for efficient domestic production, which may reduce the foreign trade ratio. Secondly, the higher per capita income may lead to an increase in demand for products and goods of particular qualities that cannot be produced at home, which may increase the foreign trade ratio. Linnemann assumes that the two effects will largely offset each other so that the foreign trade ratio should be unaffected by the country's per capita income.

34 Quoting works by i.a. Balassa,[27] Chenery,[28] Deutsch et al.[29] and Kuznets,[30] Linnemann finds good empirical evidence in support of his assumption about a negative correlation between the foreign trade ratio and the size of a country's population.

It is, however, more difficult to get empirical evidence for his assumption about the independence between the foreign trade and the country's per capita income. But the econometric studies quoted show that if per capita income has any influence at all, it is very limited. In his own empirical study he finds no significant influence of per capita income on trade.

35 We can now turn back to paragraph 30, equation (1.20) and see how Linnemann's model determines the potential trade between two countries as a function of their national products, Y_i and Y_j, and their populations, P_i and P_j.

We can also see that the trade resistance is expressed as a function of the distance, d_{ij}, and possible preferential agreements, PR, between them. What is the economic theory behind this part of the Linnemann model?

36 Linnemann makes a distinction between natural trade obstacles and artificial trade impediments.

The natural trade obstacles are divided into three groups: the costs of transportation, the time of transportation and the limited economic horizon.

The cost of transportation varies with the commodities to be transported, the distance between the countries, the kind of

---

[27]Bela Balassa, *The theory of economic integration*, Allen & Unwin, London 1962. Quotation from p. 131.

[28]Hollis B. Chenery:, "Patterns of industrial growth", *American economic Review*, vol. 50, no. 4, September 1960, pp. 624–654.

[29]Karl W. Deutsch, Chester I. Bliss and Alexander Eckstein, "Population, sovereignty and the share of foreign trade", *Economic Development and Cultural Change*, vol. 10, no. 4, July 1962, pp. 353–366.

[30]Simon Kuznets, "Economic growth of small nations", *Economic Consequences of the Size of Nations*, edited by E. A. G. Robinson, Macmillan, London 1960, pp. 14–32.

surface over which transportation is necessary, the number of reloading operations, etc. It is extremely difficult to formulate a simple expression for the trade resistance created by the costs of transportation. We can only say that the distance between the countries must be an important element of such an expression.

The time of transportation is an obstacle to trade and international water-borne transportation can take a fairly long time. This has consequences for the exchange of perishable goods; it adds an interest cost to the other costs of transportation and it makes it difficult to adjust production and sale in the importing country to rapidly changing conditions. The longer the time of transportation, the greater the inventories necessary in the importing countries. To measure the resistance to trade created by the time of transportation is not easy. But the resistance will certainly be a function of the distance between the countries concerned.

The most important natural obstacle to international trade is probably the limited economic horizon. After all, international trade is interaction between people from different countries and this interaction is not what it could be because they know too little about each other. A precise formulation of the concept economic horizon is rather difficult. We can only say that the knowledge about another country's markets for specific commodities, its language, institutions, laws and habits, will probably be smaller the farther away the country. However, we may determine the trade resistance created by a limited economic horizon, it must be a function of the distance between the countries.

We have now seen that each of the three main natural barriers to trade is determined by a multitude of factors. But each of the three barriers is highly dependent upon the distance between the countries concerned. It would make life much easier for the trade analyst if all factors other than distance would offset each other in the quantitative determination of the natural obstacles to trade. Linnemann quotes some empirical studies where such an assumption has done quite well.[31] He makes the assumption himself and he gets a reasonably good fit in his empirical analysis.

37 The artificial trade impediments are all sorts of government interference in the free flow of goods between countries. Typical examples are tariffs, quantitative restrictions and exchange controls.

Linnemann's theory of the trade restraining effects created by the artificial impediments is more a hope than a theory.

He makes the same bold assumption as Tinbergen who assumed that the effects of these restraints are normally distributed for the world at large.[32] The effects of the artificial barriers to trade between any pair of countries can therefore be divided into (i) an average trade reducing effect which is the same for all trade flows, and (ii) a random deviation from the average trade-reducing effect, thus reducing the trade flow either more or less than usual.

Linnemann concludes that the average or normal trade reducing effects of the artificial impediments are incorporated in his definition of potential foreign trade, and that the incidental or random effects (by definition) do not change the basic pattern of trade.

He has, however, to make two important exceptions. First, when trade between two countries is subject to a partial or complete embargo, or when trade is predominantly determined by political considerations, the deviations from the general pattern of trade can obviously not be considered as the result of random factors. This problem is solved by Linnemann by excluding trade with Communist countries from the analyses.

[31]The quotations are made on p. 29 in Hans Linnemann, *op. cit.* Among the works quoted are: "Der Güterverkehr der Weltwirtschaft", *Vierteljahrshefte zur Statistik des Deutschen Reichs*, Ergänzungsheft zu Heft 1928, I, Statistiches Reichsamt, Berlin 1928, and G. J. Aeyelts Avernik, *De gevolgen van de Europamarkt voor de intra-Europese handel*, Netherlands Economic Institute, Rotterdam 1960–1961.

[32]See paragraph 27.

Secondly, it may prove impossible to explain the effects of preferential trade arrangements like those within the British Commonwealth, the French Community, the European Economic Community, etc., as random deviations from a world pattern of trade. Such preferential arrangements may have systematic trade increasing effects. This problem is solved by introducing into the basic model a specific variable, PR, for preferential trade arrangements.

38   Summing up, we can say that Linnemann's main contribution is his explanation of the concept potential foreign trade. Far better than his predecessors in the school of Social Physics, he has been able to present an economic theory behind this concept.

He has, however, not been able to present any convincing economic theory behind the concept, trade resistance. The theory behind this concept is still either an analogy from physics or a combination of a good hope and a tolerable statistical fit.

Conclusions

39   The theories surveyed in this chapter all try to explain why nations (or regions) trade. But they are very different. Let's mention three fundamental differences.

First, the Heckscher–Ohlin and the Burenstam Linder models determine the composition of trade, i.e., which commodities are imported and exported, whereas the models from the school of Social Physics determine the volume of trade, i.e., how many commodities are imported and exported.

This does not mean that conventional economic theory cannot explain the volume of trade. A comprehensive general equilibrium model can do the job. Neither does it mean that a member of the school of Social Physics cannot explain the composition of trade. An analysis of differences in technology and factor prices can help him. But in both cases the analyst has to leave his main field of interest in the theory of international trade.

Secondly, the Heckscher–Ohlin model assumes away the friction of distance, whereas the school of Social Physics makes this friction one of the main determinants of interregional and international trade.

Thirdly, the Heckscher–Ohlin model assumes that production functions are the same all over the world, whereas Burenstam Linder and the members of the school of Social Physics assume that production functions differ between regions and between nations. Heckscher and Ohlin assume that comparative advantages are due to differences in relative factor endowments, i.e., given by nature, whereas Burenstam Linder and the social physicists assume that comparative advantages are due to differences in technologies, i.e., man-made.

40 In the model to be constructed in chapter 3 we shall integrate some of the basic elements of the models surveyed above.

From the Heckscher–Ohlin model we shall use the interdependence between trade and relative commodity prices.

From the Burenstam Linder model and the models in Social Physics we shall use the spatial differences in production functions.

From the social physics models we shall further use the friction of distance as an important explanatory variable.

The way in which these elements are integrated in our model is, however, to a great extent determined by the way in which different theories answer question number two: "How does trade affect the international distribution of income?".

CHAPTER 2

How does trade affect the international distribution of income?

1 This important question has been answered by the Heckscher–Ohlin school, by the school of Social Physics and by Gunnar Myrdal.

The Heckscher–Ohlin school has analysed the influence of commodity trade upon the prices of the factors of production. It comes to the conclusion that free trade in commodities will lead to a more or less perfect equalization of factor prices and thereby to a more equal international (or interregional) distribution of income.[1]

The school of Social Physics has an approach most different to that of the Heckscher–Ohlin school. The members of this school are interested in the so-called macro-concept of income per capita and not in the different components of this income. The conclusions of the two schools are, however, very close to each other. Both schools believe that trade will lead towards an equalization of the geographical distribution of income, although they have different reasons for believing so.

Like the school of Social Physics, *Gunnar Myrdal* is more interested in the concept of income per capita than in its different components. But unlike both the above mentioned schools, Myrdal does not believe that the liberalization of trade will lead to a more equal distribution of income between nations or regions. On the contrary, he fears that the market mechanism,

---

[1] If factor prices are equalized, the only possible differences between nations (or regions) in incomes per capita are those to be explained by differences in the amount of capital per inhabitant or by differences in labour force participation rates.

left to itself, may make the rich countries (or regions) richer and the poor countries (or regions) poorer.[2]

In this chapter, we shall present the basic thought behind the three answers given to the question of how trade affects the international distribution of income.

The Heckscher–Ohlin school

2   The members of the Heckscher–Ohlin school very often present their thoughts in a three step analysis.

Firstly, they make clear the very strict assumptions of their model.

Secondly, they show how free trade under these assumptions must lead to full equalization of national or regional factor prices.

Thirdly, they agree that their assumptions may be unrealistic. Some of these assumptions are therefore relaxed and it is shown that this does not really matter. The factor price equalization theorem needs only slight modifications.

We shall now see how this could be done.

3   The assumptions of the Heckscher–Ohlin model were exposed in chapter 1, paragraph 2. We shall, however, repeat them here because we want to divide them into three groups.

In the first group we shall have the assumptions about the *pattern of production*. It is assumed that each country, I and II, produces both commodities, X and Y.

In the second group we shall have the assumptions about the *production functions*. It is assumed that both factors, capital (K) and labour (L), are needed in the production of each commodity. The marginal rate of substitution between factors is assumed to be increasing in the production of each commodity, i.e., isoquants are convex to the origin. It is further assumed that

[2]See Gunnar Myrdal, *Economic theory and underdeveloped regions*, Duckworth & Co., London 1957.

production functions are identical in the two countries and that they are linear and homogeneous. Finally, it is assumed that at any given factor price ratio, the ratio of capital to labour will be higher in the production of X than in the production of Y, i.e., that X will always be the most capital-intensive good and Y the most labour-intensive good.

In the third group we shall have the assumptions about the *interdependence of the national markets*. In each country, perfect competition is assumed both in the markets for commodities and in the markets for factors of production. Commodities can move freely between nations, i.e., there are no barriers to trade and no costs of transportation, but capital and labour are assumed to be internationally immobile and in fixed supply.

This grouping of the assumptions is made to facilitate the presentation of the second step and the third step of the Heckscher–Ohlin school analysis.

4 We now turn to the *proof of the factor price equalization theorem.*

Here it might be useful to introduce *Kelvin Lancaster's concept of corresponding points.*[3]

In fig. 2.1 the box diagram O_xEFG shows the factor endowments of the relatively capital-rich country I. O_x is the origin of the X-isoquant map and F is the origin of the Y-isoquant map.

The box diagram FLO_yK shows the factor endowments of the relatively labour-rich country II. Capital and labour are measured in the same units as in country I. F is the origin of the X-isoquant map and O_y is the origin of the Y-isoquant map.

The total world supply of capital can be represented by the distance O_xO or HO_y and the total world supply of labour by the distance O_xH or OO_y. The rectangle O_xOO_yH can be considered as a box diagram showing the world's total endowment of

[3]See Kelvin Lancaster, "The Heckscher–Ohlin trade model: a geometric treatment", *Economica*, 37th year, New Series, vol. 24, no. 94, February 1957, pp. 19–39.

capital and labour. In this world box diagram O_x is the origin of the X-isoquant map and O_y is the origin of the Y-isoquant map.

We now choose a point P′ on the contract curve of country I and we draw the straight lines connecting P′ with O_x and F respectively.

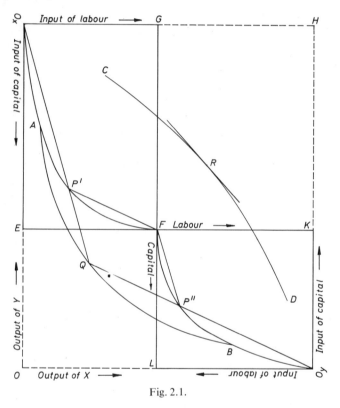

Fig. 2.1.

Through F we draw a line FP″ parallel to O_xP′ and through O_y we draw a line O_yP″ parallel to FP′. The two lines intersect at P″.

If P′ was chosen between A and F on country I's contract curve,[4] then P″ will lie inside country II's box diagram and P′ and P″ will be called a pair of corresponding points.

[4] A is the point where the (not drawn) produced diagonal O_yF of country II's box diagram intersects country I's contract curve.

5 We may now ask: Given the assumptions exposed in paragraph 3 above, what can we tell about corresponding points?

The first group of assumptions does not tell much except that factor allocations indicated by corresponding points can be studied without violating the constraint demanding that both commodities be produced in each country,[5] which is important to know, but not very interesting.

6 The second group of assumptions enables us to show that each of the corresponding points are located upon a national contract curve.

We know that P' is a point on the contract curve of country I in fig. 2.1. This implies that in point P' the slope of the tangent to the X-isoquant is equal to the slope of the tangent to the Y-isoquant.

We assumed that production functions were identical in the two countries and homogeneous of degree one. This implies that the slope of the tangents to the X-isoquants along FP" is constant and equal to the slope of the tangents to the X-isoquants along O_xP'Q. Similarly, the slope of the tangents to the Y-isoquants along O_yP"Q is constant and equal to the slope of the tangents to the Y-isoquants along FP'.

Therefore, in P" the slope of the tangent to the X-isoquant must be equal to the slope of the tangent to the Y-isoquant. This means that P" is a point on country II's contract curve.

7 The third group of assumptions makes it possible to draw the very important conclusions, that if the national allocations of factors are indicated by a pair of corresponding points, then (a) the absolute factor prices and (b) the relative commodity prices will be the same in the two countries.

[5]For the moment we shall neglect the problems arising from different definitions of the concept of corresponding points. In our definition we demanded that P' should be chosen on country I's contract curve between A and F, i.e., excluding A and F. The concept has, however, also been defined including A and F in the set of possible locations for P', see e.g. William Penfield Travis, *The theory of trade and protection*, Harvard Economic Studies, vol. 121, Cambridge, Mass. 1964, p. 14.

7a We have assumed perfect competition on the national markets for factors and commodities. This implies (1) that each factor is paid the value of its marginal product and (2) that the value of a factor's marginal product is the same in both industries.

The second implication means that we can limit our analysis to one of the industries. We shall choose the X-industry.

The question is now: What determines the marginal product of a factor, e.g. labour, in the production of commodity X?

The answer is: The capital–labour ratio in the X-industry and only the capital–labour ratio. This answer can be given because we know (from the second group of assumptions) that production functions are homogeneous of degree one.

In fig. 2.1, the capital–labour ratio in the X-industry of country I is expressed by the slope of the straight line O_xP'. The capital–labour ratio in the X-industry of country II is expressed by the slope of the straight line FP'' which is parallel to O_xP'. So, the capital–labour ratio is the same in the two X-industries and since production functions are identical we conclude that the marginal product of labour is the same in the two countries.

For the same reasons, the marginal product of capital will be the same in the two countries.

This leads us to the conclusion that the absolute factor prices will be the same in country I and country II.

7b The assumption of perfect competition on the national markets for factors and commodities implies (1) that the ratio between a factor's marginal products in the two industries will be the same for both factors and (2) that the relative commodity prices are determined by this ratio.

From section 7a above we know that the marginal products of capital and labour are the same in the two countries. Therefore, the ratio between a factor's marginal products in the two industries cannot differ internationally. And therefore, relative commodity prices will be the same in country I and country II.

8 It is now very easy to prove the factor price equalization theorem.

Given the assumptions of group three, especially the absence of transportation costs and other barriers to international commodity movements, we can conclude that trade will lead to an equalization of relative commodity prices.

Given the assumptions of group two (about the production functions) and the assumptions of group one (about the pattern of production), we know that every pair of relative commodity prices determines one and only one point on each of the national contract curves and that these two contract curve points will be a pair of corresponding points.

We can therefore conclude that free trade in commodities will lead to a full international equalization of factor prices.

This is, in short, the Heckscher–Ohlin theory of how trade affects the international distribution of income.

9 Having proved the factor price equalization theorem, we now turn to the relaxation of the assumptions of the Heckscher–Ohlin model. We shall try to relax one important assumption in each of the three groups and see what happens to the factor price equalization theorem.

Relaxing the first group of assumptions, we shall allow for specialization of production and ask whether factor prices can be expected to differ internationally because one or both of the countries specialize their production.

The answer to this question is: not necessarily. Traditional international trade theory assumes that each country produces both commodities, because such an assumption is convenient for many purposes, not because it is a necessary condition for factor price equalization.

After all, the factor price equalization theorem can be proved if (1) each pair of relative commodity prices determines one and only one factor allocation point on each of the national contract curves, (2) the slope of the tangent to the isoquants is the same in these two national contract curve points, and (3) the capital–

labour ratios in the production of X and Y do not differ inter-nationally.

Fig. 2.2 shows how these conditions can be fulfilled under specialization.

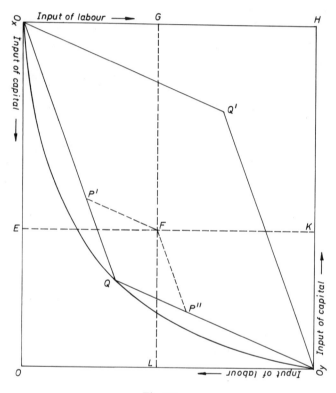

Fig. 2.2.

10   In fig. 2.2 the box diagram O_xOO_yH shows the total factor endowments of the world. The convex curve O_xQO_y is the world contract curve and the point Q indicates the allocation of factors between industries in an undivided world.

We now assume that the world is divided into two countries.

Each country gets a share of the world's factor endowments, but the total allocation of factors between industries is unchanged. It is still indicated by the point Q.

Fig. 2.2 shows a case where country I gets the factor endowments illustrated by the box diagram O_xEFG and country II the one illustrated by FLO_yK. But the point of division, F, could be located anywhere in the world box diagram.

The location of F will decide whether factor prices will be equalized or not. We shall now see that equalization will take place if F is located inside or upon the boundaries of the parallelogram O_xQO_yQ'.

11 If F is located inside the parallelogram, factor prices must be equalized because it is always possible to find a pair of corresponding points like P' and P'' in fig. 2.2. In this case both countries will produce both commodities.

If F is located on one of the boundaries, but not in point Q or point Q', factor prices must also be equalized. One of the countries must specialize and the other produce both commodities. If F, e.g., lies between O_x and Q', country I will specialize in the production of Y, while country II will produce both X and Y. Factor price equalization will be ensured because the capital–labour ratio in country I's Y-industry (the slope of O_xQ') is equal to the capital–labour ratio of country II's Y-industry.

If F is located at point Q or point Q', both countries will specialize. A location at Q means that country I will specialize in the production of X and country II in the production of Y. A location at Q' gives the opposite result. But in both cases factor prices will be equalized. Both at point Q and point Q', the X-isoquant of the X producing country's X-isoquant map is tangent to the Y-isoquant of the Y producing country's Y-isoquant map. This will ensure equalization of relative factor prices. The absolute factor prices will, however, also be equalized because there will be no international differences in the capital–labour ratios in the production of X and Y.

If F is located outside the parallelogram O_xQO_yQ' factor prices will not be equalized. In such a case, it would not be possible to obtain the world factor allocation indicated by Q without getting different national capital–labour ratios in one of the industries.

12   In a 1964 book[6] William Penfield Travis called a parallelogram like O_xQO_yQ' an equalization region. The boundaries of an equalization region were called specialization boundaries.

We have now seen that trade may equalize factor prices even in cases where both countries specialize their production. We have also seen that factor prices will be equalized only if the point of division F is located in the equalization region. We shall therefore reformulate our question from paragraph 9 above and ask: "Can factor prices be expected to differ between nations because F is located outside the equalization region?"

13   Travis[7] has tried to answer this question by comparing the area of the equalization region with that of the world box diagram. The ratio between these two areas was called the likelihood of complete factor price equalization.

Fig. 2.2 shows a case where the likelihood is relatively great. Q is located in the middle of the contract curve. This gives a larger equalization region than if Q had been located near to O_x or O_y. The contract curve bends relatively far away from the diagonal of the box. This is due to the relatively great differences in the factor intensities of X and Y. If these differences had been smaller, the contract curve would have been closer to the diagonal and the area of the equalization region would also have been smaller.

But even if the likelihood of factor price equalization is relatively great in the case illustrated by fig. 2.2, it is not impressive. So, in a world without international factor movements, we

[6]William Penfield Travis, *The theory of trade and protection*, Harvard Economic Studies, vol. 121, Cambridge, Mass. 1964, p. 18.
[7]William Penfield Travis, *op. cit.*, pp. 19, 22 and 39.

should doubt whether free trade in commodities would lead
to an equalization of factor prices.

It is, however, much more pleasant to doubt the absence of
international factor movements. Limited capital movements
might in many cases be sufficient to bring F into the equalization region.

Allowing for such capital movements, the Heckscher–Ohlin
school can conclude: "It is rather unlikely that factor prices
should differ between nations because F is located outside the
equalization region."

14 Turning to the assumptions about production functions,
we shall see what happens to the factor price equalization
theorem when we allow for factor intensity cross-overs.

Fig. 2.3 shows a simple case of factor intensity cross-overs.
The two representative isoquants are tangent to each other at
point T. At the relative factor prices expressed by the common

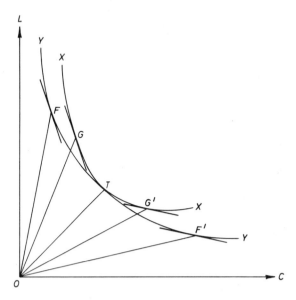

Fig. 2.3.

slope of the two isoquants at T, the factor intensity will be the same in both industries, i.e., equal to the slope of OT.

At relative factor prices expressed by slopes of tangents to the isoquants "northwest" of T, e.g., those expressed by the common slope of the tangents in F and G, commodity X will be relatively capital-intensive and commodity Y relatively labour-intensive.

At relative prices expressed by slopes of tangents to the isoquants "southeast" of T, e.g., those expressed by the common slope of the tangents in F' and G', commodity X will be relatively labour-intensive and commodity Y relatively capital-intensive.

15   Factor intensity cross-overs may, however, take place more than once. This is illustrated in fig. 2.4 which was developed by Harry G. Johnson[8] on the basis of a diagram by R. F. Harrod.

The top half of the diagram shows the optimal capital–labour ratios, r_x and r_y, in the production of each good, X and Y, at different relative factor prices. The relative factor prices are expressed as the price, w, of labour in terms of capital. Factor intensity cross-overs will take place at w_a and w_b. Commodity X will be the capital-intensive good when $w < w_a$ or $w > w_b$. But if $w_a < w < w_b$ the capital-intensive good will be Y.

The bottom half of the diagram shows the functional relationship between relative factor prices and relative commodity prices. This is done by depicting C_y, the price of commodity Y in terms of commodity X, as a function of w, the relative price of labour. Fig. 2.4 illustrates how C_y must move in the same direction as w, when Y is the labour-intensive good, and in the opposite direction, when Y is the capital-intensive good.

[8]See Harry G. Johnson, "Factor endowments, international trade and factor prices", *The Manchester School of Economic and Social Studies*, vol. 25, no. 3, September 1957, pp. 270–283, reprinted in Harry G. Johnson, *International trade and economic growth*, Allen & Unwin, London 1958, pp. 17–30. See esp. pp. 18–19.

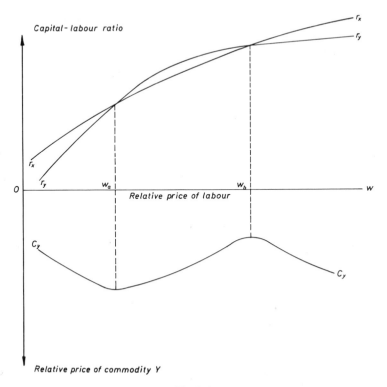

Fig. 2.4.

16   We now assume that country I has an over-all capital–labour ratio r_I as shown in fig. 2.5. Before trade is established, country I uses most of its resources in the production of the labour-intensive commodity Y. This results in a relatively high price w_I of labour and a relatively high price C_I of commodity Y.

We then assume that country II has the over-all capital–labour ratio r_{II} and that this country before trade uses most of its resources in the production of the labour-intensive commodity X. The result is a relatively high price w_{II} of labour and a relatively low price C_{II} of commodity Y.

When trade is opened up, commodity prices are equalized. The relative price of Y will be C_e in both countries. Country I will import Y and shift resources from the labour-intensive Y-industry to the capital-intensive X-industry. This will reduce the relative price of labour from w_I to w_{Ie}.

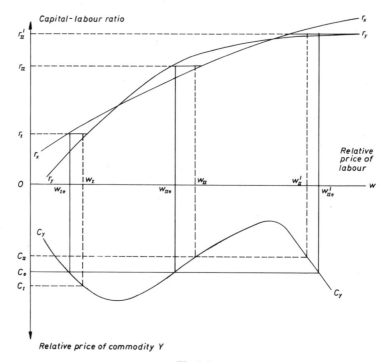

Fig. 2.5.

Country II will import X and shift resources from the labour-intensive X-industry to the capital-intensive Y-industry. This will reduce the relative price of labour from w_{II} to w_{IIe}.

Trade has thus resulted in a reduction of the relative price of labour in both countries. Whether this will widen or narrow the national differences in factor prices depends upon the circumstances.

17 The preceding paragraph dealt with a case of one factor-intensity cross-over. Suppose that the over-all capital–labour ratio of country II had been r'_{II} instead of r_{II}. We would then have a case of two factor-intensity cross-overs.

In this case country II will import X and shift resources from the capital-intensive X-industry to the labour-intensive Y-industry. This will increase the relative price of labour from w'_{II} to w'_{IIe}.

We remember that the relative price of labour in country I was reduced from w_I to w_{Ie}. Trade has thus widened the gap between the relative prices of labour in the two countries.

18 The case with one factor-intensity cross-over gives the same result as cases with an odd number of cross-overs and the case with two factor-intensity cross-overs yields the same result as cases with an even number of cross-overs.

19 We can now conclude that in a world without international factor movements, factor-intensity cross-overs mean that relative factor prices will not be equalized and that national differences may even be widened by the opening up of trade.

The Heckscher–Ohlin school would, however, not be inclined to expect national differences in factor prices due to factor-intensity cross-overs. It would prefer to allow for some international capital movements which would change the two countries' capital–labour ratios, thereby eliminating factor-intensity cross-overs.

20 Finally, we shall relax the assumptions about the interdependence of the national markets by allowing for transportation costs.

This is done in a simple analysis where it is assumed that commodity X can be used for two purposes. It can be consumed directly or it can be used for international transportation of commodities.

Fig. 2.6 is a diagram like fig. 2.5, but it has no factor-intensity cross-overs. Throughout, X is the capital-intensive good while Y is the labour-intensive good.

The situation before trade is characterized by the relative commodity prices C_I and C_{II} and by the relative factor prices w_I and w_{II}.

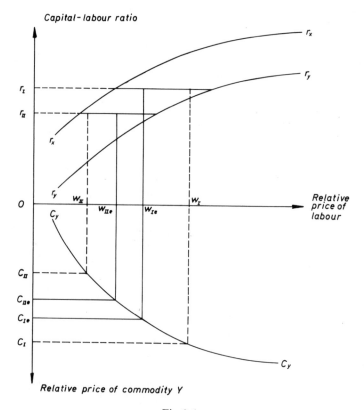

Fig. 2.6.

Due to the costs of transportation, the opening up of trade will not lead to an equalization of commodity prices. The new equilibrium prices of Y in terms of X will be C_{Ie} and C_{IIe} respectively. Country I will import Y from country II and $(C_{Ie} - C_{IIe})$

will be the amount of X it takes to ship the marginal unit of commodity Y to country I from country II.

When trade does not equalize commodity prices it does not equalize factor prices either. But the difference between national factor prices is narrowed by trade $(w_{Ie} - w_{IIe}) < (w_I - w_{II})$. The introduction of transportation costs can therefore only modify the results of the Heckscher–Ohlin analysis.

21 We have now relaxed one important assumption from each of the three groups organized in paragraph 2 above. We have seen how this creates difficulties for the factor price equalization theorem and how such difficulties may be overcome by allowing for some, but not necessarily free, international capital movements and by modifying the results of the Heckscher–Ohlin analysis. We could go on relaxing other assumptions of the model but this would not get us much further.

We shall therefore conclude by saying that the Heckscher–Ohlin school is aware of the limitations of the model predicting complete factor price equalization as a result of free international trade. But it believes that national differences in factor prices would be reduced if trade were liberalized and international capital movements were permitted.

The Social Physics school

22 The basic thought of the Social Physics school is expressed in two books by William Warntz.

The first book, *Toward a geography of price*,[9] was published in 1959. For 4 standard agricultural commodities, it shows how prices paid to farmers in the different American states may vary due to the friction of distance. From our point of view, this book is interesting because it focuses upon the friction of distance which the Heckscher–Ohlin school started by assuming

[9]William Warntz, *Toward a geography of price*, University of Pennsylvania Press, Philadelphia, Penn. 1959.

away, cf. the assumptions about the interdependence of the national (or regional) markets for commodities.

The second book, *Macrogeography and income fronts*,[10] was published in 1965. It shows how the regional income differentials in the United States from 1880 to 1956 could be explained by the friction of distance and how the friction of distance could be explained by the well-known fact that spatial adjustment processes take time. From our point of view, the book is interesting not only because it deals with regional income differences, but also because it gives a new interpretation of the friction of distance, because it builds this concept into a dynamic model of interaction between spatially separated economic units and because the dynamic analysis leads to conclusions very similar to those of the static Heckscher–Ohlin analysis.

In the following we shall give a short survey of each of the two books.

23   Warntz's 1959 book examines the prices paid (at the farm) to American farmers for wheat, potatoes, onions and strawberries during the ten-year period 1940–1949. For all four commodities, the average prices by states vary considerably and this variation is explained by the friction of distance.

The costs of transportation are thought to be essential to the friction of distance, but great importance is also attached to lack of information and other market imperfections.

Warntz believes that the friction of distance will influence both the demand for, and the supply of a given commodity in a given state.

24   The friction of distance means that the demand for a given commodity becomes relatively stronger in a state close to the centre of the national market and relatively weaker in a state in the periphery of the national market for the commodity.

[10]William Warntz, *Macrogeography and income fronts*, Monograph Series, no. 3, Regional Science Research Institute, Philadelphia, Penn. 1965.

For all four commodities studied by Warntz, a state is said to be close to the national market if it has a high *gross economic population potential*.

The gross economic population potential $_iV$ of the state i is defined by the formula:

$$_iV = \sum_{j=1}^{n} \frac{(Y_j/P_j)P_j}{d_{ij}}. \tag{2.1}$$

This formula is a slight variation of Stewart's formula (1.4) for the total demographic potential at i. The difference between the two formulae is that Warntz has found it appropriate to weigh populations with per capita income. Even in an analysis of the U.S. market for food, purchasing power is more important than the mere size of population.

Fig. 2.7 gives a map of the gross economic population potentials which were used in Warntz's analyses.

25 The friction of distance further means that the *supply* of a given commodity becomes relatively stronger in a state close to the centre of the national production and relatively weaker in a state far from the centre of the national production of the commodity.

A state is said to be near to the national centre of production if it has a high *product supply space potential*.

The product supply space potential $_iS$ for a given commodity in a given state i is defined by:

$$_iS = \sum_{j=1}^{n} \frac{O_j}{d_{ij}}, \tag{2.2}$$

where O_j is the output of the commodity in the state j. Formula (2.2) is a slight variant of Stewart's formula (1.4) for the total demographic potential at i. The only difference between the two formulae is that Warntz is interested in commodities where Stewart was interested in human beings.

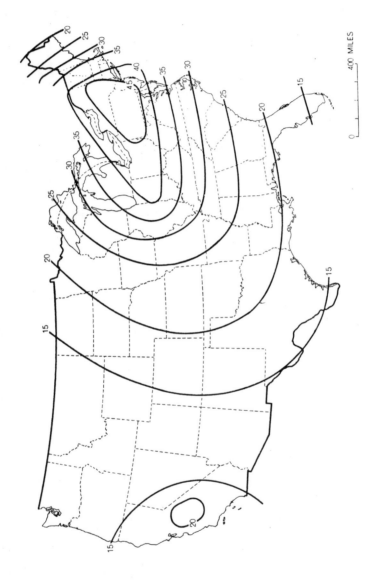

Fig. 2.7. United States annual gross economic population potential (1940–1949 average), in billions of dollars per hundred miles. From: William Warntz, *Toward a geography of price*, University of Pennsylvania Press, Philadelphia, Penn. 1959, p. 67.

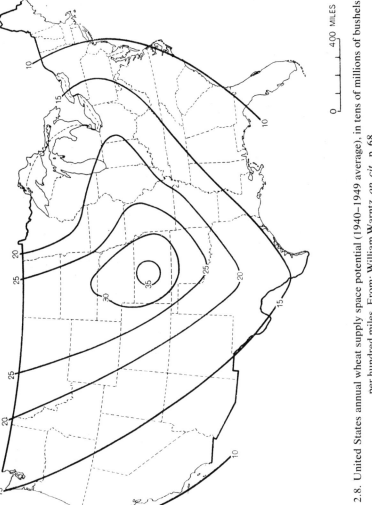

Fig. 2.8. United States annual wheat supply space potential (1940–1949 average), in tens of millions of bushels per hundred miles. From: William Warntz, *op. cit.*, p. 68.

Fig. 2.8 brings a map of the wheat supply space potential which Warntz used in his analysis.

26   The output of agricultural products like wheat, potatoes, onions and strawberries will emerge during short harvest periods determined by climatic conditions, etc. But the harvest periods will be different in the different American states because the climate is different. The national output of a given commodity will therefore emerge over a period called the national harvest period which is longer than a state harvest period.

The national output of the commodity in question may be different in different parts of the national harvest period. This will influence the state supplies of the commodity.

The friction of distance will mean that the supply of the commodity becomes relatively stronger in a state whose harvest period is close to the peak of the national harvest period and relatively weaker in a state whose harvest period is far from the peak of the national harvest period for the commodity.

A state's harvest period is said to be close to the peak of the national harvest period if the state has a high *product supply time potential.*

The state product supply time potential is computed on the basis of the *national product supply time potential* which for the middle of the month m is called $_mT$ and defined by

$$_mT = \sum_{n=1}^{12} \frac{O^n}{d_{mn}} + \sum_{n=1}^{12} \frac{O^n}{d_{mn*}}, \qquad n \neq m, \tag{2.3}$$

where $O^n =$ the national output of the commodity during the
$\qquad\qquad$ nth month.

$\qquad$ $d_{mn} =$ the distance between the middle of the mth month
$\qquad\qquad$ and the middle of the following nth month.

$\qquad$ $d_{mn*} =$ the distance between the middle of the mth month
$\qquad\qquad$ and the middle of the past nth month.

If, for example, the mth month is April and the nth month June, d_{mn} will be 2 months and d_{mn*} 10 months.

Formula (2.3) can be regarded as a sum of two potentials *ad modum* formula (1.4). One of these is focused upon the peak of the past national harvest period and the other upon the peak of the coming national harvest period. The economic theory behind this construction is that the supply of a commodity will reflect both past production and an anticipated future production of the commodity.

Having computed the national product supply time potentials for the middle of each of the twelve months of the year, Warntz plots his results into a diagram like fig. 2.9, and connects the twelve points by free hand. This gives him a national product supply time potential curve.

The *state product supply time potential* for a given product and a given state is then defined as the national product supply time potential on the average harvest date for the product in the state.

Fig. 2.9 shows the national onion supply time potentials used by Warntz. The onion supply time potential for, e.g., the state Utah can be read from the curve of fig. 2.9 when we know the average harvest date for onions in Utah. Warntz tells us that

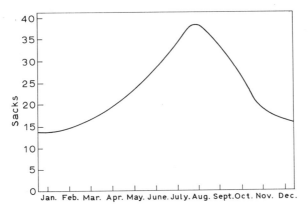

Fig. 2.9. United States onion supply time potentials (1940–1949 average), in millions of sacks (fifty pounds each) per month. From: William Warntz, *op. cit.*, p. 73.

the average harvest date is the 15th September which gives Utah an onion supply time potential of 33.0 million sacks per month;[11] cf. fig. 2.9.

27   *Warntz's conclusion* was that the friction of distance should lead to geographical variations in the prices paid to farmers and that *prices should be expected to vary directly with gross economic population potential and inversely with product supply space potential and product supply time potential.*

This hypothesis was tested in a multiple linear regression analysis for each of the four commodities studied. The coefficients of multiple correlation were 0.86 for wheat, 0.79 for onions, 0.69 for potatoes and 0.69 for strawberries. These results were not impressive, but they were not bad either.

28   We now turn to Warntz's 1965 book, *Macrogeography and income fronts*. This book is, in fact, most different from the first one. The *Geography of price* tries to explain a limited problem and it does so in a way which makes good sense to an economist. The regional price differences are predominantly explained by economic arguments.

Macrogeography and income fronts takes a very broad look at the world and the conclusions are to an alarming extent based upon analogies from the natural sciences.

This broad look at the world is rather fascinating. The book starts with an analysis of the regional income differences in the United States from 1880 to 1956. It is shown how these differences have diminished over time and they are predicted to disappear around the close of the present century, as a result of spatial interaction. After a somewhat longer period of time, the international differences in per capita income are also supposed to disappear. Warntz therefore concludes with some remarks about the balance of power in such a world.

[11]See William Warntz, *op. cit.*, table IV, p. 52, table XIII, p. 77 and table XVII, p. 81.

The analogies from the natural sciences are, however, most difficult for an economist to accept. He may ask himself whether he is reading science or science fiction. He may be shocked by some of the assumptions implicitly made by Warntz and he may be tempted to dismiss the whole book, but he should not.

Instead he should mobilize all his patience and try to produce an economic interpretation. This is our intention here.

We should especially like to regard the two books as parts of one and the same economic explanation of spatial interaction. In this context, we should like to say that the 1959 book told us that the friction of distance should be taken into account in an analysis of interaction between spatially separated economic units, while the 1965 book told us how this could be done in a dynamic model.

Partial to this interpretation, we may not always be fair to Warntz. Those who want precise information about Warntz's thoughts should therefore read his book themselves.

29 The 1965 book presents an economic model in time and space. The model will, left to itself, work towards an equilibrium where per capita income is the same in all regions. Existing regional income differences will always be gradually diminished by the market mechanism. But this process takes time.

Let us assume that exogenous factors created regional income differentials at time t_0. These differences were pronounced at time t_1 and less pronounced at time t_2 but still of importance. The reduction of the regional income differences simply reflects that the spatial adjustment process has been working for a longer time at t_2 than at t_1.

If we explain the regional income differences by the friction of distance, as does Warntz, we come to the conclusion that the friction of distance is greater at time t_1 than at time t_2. We could also say that the friction of distance diminishes over time or that the friction of distance is a function of the time needed by the relevant spatial adjustment processes. In the case studied by Warntz, the adjustment process takes one and a half centuries.

30   The empirical study of the 1965 book shows that the United States could be divided into three per capita income regions. To Warntz, this is a consequence of two major events which took place about the middle of the 19th century. The first of these events was the mineral discoveries which created a high-income area in the Far West. The second event was the Civil War which created a low-income area in the South. Since the Civil War, no corresponding events have, according to Warntz, created new disequilibria and an adjustment process has been going on.

31   The first step in Warntz's analysis is the delineation of the income regions. This is done for each of the years 1880, 1890, 1900, 1910, 1920, 1930, 1940, 1950, 1956 and 1959.

It is assumed that the American states can be divided into three groups: high per capita income states, medium per capita income states and low per capita income states.

It is further assumed that within each group of states there is a positive correlation between per capita income and state income potential. The income potential is defined by formula (2.1), cf. paragraph 24 above, letting Y_j stand for total disposable personal income in state j. The economic theory behind this assumption could be that the income potential will be relatively high in the urbanized regions and that urbanization due to agglomeration economies might increase per capita income.

Finally, it is assumed that if the log of each state's per capita disposable personal income is plotted against the log of its income potential in a diagram like fig. 2.10, it is possible to fit the data to three parallel regression lines, one for each income group.

What Warntz has to do is therefore to try to determine the three regression lines.

He starts by trying to fit all the data of fig. 2.10 to one line. This gives him, of course, a very poor correlation coefficient. He then eliminates the state data showing the greatest deviations from his regression line. A new set of computations gives him a new regression line and a better correlation coefficient. If this is not satisfactory, further elimination takes place and the process goes on until he has got a reasonably high correlation coefficient.

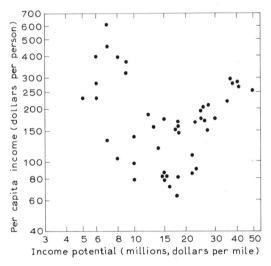

Fig. 2.10. Per capita income and income potential in the United States 1880 (by states). From: William Warntz, *Macrogeography and income fronts*, Philadelphia, Penn. 1965, fig. 8, p. 41.

The straight line A in fig. 2.11 is the result of such operations. The data denoted by the large dots are those which remained in the analysis, while the data denoted by the small dots were eliminated. The straight lines B and C are placed 3 standard errors of estimation above and below the main regression line.

The large dot states in fig. 2.11. are now referred to the medium per capita income group. The states represented by the small dots in the upper left corner of the diagram are referred to the high per capita income group and the straight line E, parallel to A, is fitted to the data. Correspondingly, the states of the lower right corner of fig. 2.11 are referred to the low per capita income group and the straight line D, parallel to A, is fitted to the data.

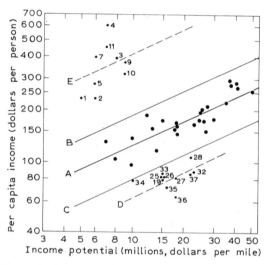

Fig. 2.11. Per capita income and income potential in the United States 1880 (by states). From: William Warntz, *op. cit.*, fig. 9, p. 42.

Fig. 2.12 shows that the high-income states are located in the Far West, the low-income states in the South and the medium-income states in what Warntz calls the main sequence.

32   For all the years studied, Warntz succeeds in isolating the three groups of data from each other. Some of the states may at different points of time belong to different per capita income groups, but the general picture remains unchanged with high incomes in the Far West and low incomes in the South.

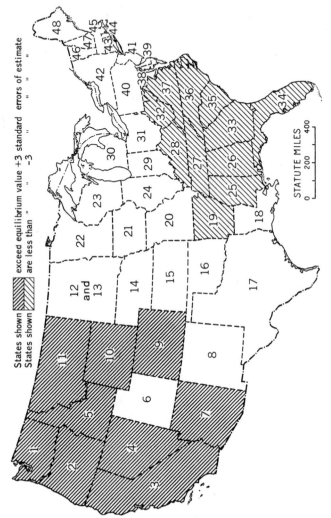

Fig. 2.12. 1880 per capita income regions in the United States, based on correlation with income potential. From: William Warntz, *op. cit.*, fig. 10, p. 44. (State numbers refer to those in the original text.)

33   The second step in Warntz's analysis is the presentation of a theory for the equalization of per capita income as a result of spatial interaction.

At first glance, it looks as if Warntz's theory is based upon a rather doubtful analogy from the macroscopic gas laws of Boyle and Gay Lussac. He says that per capita income could be regarded as a magnitude like temperature and he regards an income map such as fig. 2.12 above as something like a weather map. The high-income areas are regarded as areas with high temperature, the low-income areas as areas with low temperature and the medium per capita income areas as areas with "normal" temperature. The frontiers which separate states belonging to different income groups are called "income fronts" in analogy to the hot and cold fronts of the daily weather map. The equalization of per capita income is then regarded as a process following the meteorological laws of the dissipation of hot and cold fronts. The result is a rather meaningless economic theory based upon at least two unrealistic assumptions. One is that the equalization of per capita income is mainly the consequence of migrations. The other is that the income potentials remain absolutely unchanged, despite the migrations. This will be the case only if the marginal productivity of migrants is zero in the states which they leave and zero in the states to which they go. No economist would find such an assumption reasonable.

34   A more careful reading of Warntz's 1965 book might, however, provide the economist with ideas and arguments upon which he could build a meaningful economic theory.

He might, e.g., accept Warntz's three basic assumptions: (a) that the initial regional income differences are results of external disturbances (i.e., the mineral discoveries and the Civil War) of a general interregional equilibrium; (b) that the disequilibrium thus created leads to a number of spatial adjustment processes aiming at establishing a new general interregional equilibrium without pronounced regional income differences; (c) that these adjustment processes take considerable time.

The acceptance of assumptions (b) and (c) leads to the conclusion that if no new disturbances occur, then the regional income differences will diminish over time. At any given point of time such differences are regarded as functions of the friction of distance. Therefore, it can be said that the friction of distance diminishes over time or that the friction of distance simply reflects that spatial adjustment processes take time. But what is the economic theory behind assumption (b)?

35 First of all some sort of a Heckscher–Ohlin theory: Warntz does not believe that *trade* will equalize commodity prices, cf. his *Geography of price*, but he believes that interregional trade may bring prices closer to each other and that this may work towards equalization of factor remunerations.

Warntz also believes in the equalizing effects of factor movements, especially migrations of labour. But he regards such migrations as determined not only by wage differentials but also by the information available to the labour force. The more a person knows about real wages and living conditions in the different regions, the more willing he will be to move from a low-income region to a high-income region. And a person's knowledge about another region depends upon the general level of information, his own education and how many of his friends or relatives have already moved to that region. Further, Warntz believes that the volume of migrations is determined by the age structure of the population. Younger people are supposed to be more willing to move than older people.

The third main equalizing factor in which Warntz believes is the federal budget. He says that progressive income taxation will lower disposable personal income most in the high-income regions, whereas the low-income regions will benefit most from the social welfare programmes.

36   We have now seen how Warntz has delineated the income regions and how he has presented a theory according to which the regional income differences should diminish over time. We shall then turn to the third step of his analysis and see how he tries to verify his theory.

The verification is done in two rather similar ways. Firstly, he compares the regression lines for each of the years studied in diagrams like fig. 2.11. This comparison shows that the regression lines move closer to each other during the period under consideration, or that the income differences between regions have been reduced. The comparison also shows a gradual reduction of the slopes of the regression lines, or that the income differences within regions have diminished.

Secondly, Warntz presents a table like table 2.1 showing the per capita income of each of the three regions as a percentage of the per capita income of the main sequence.

TABLE 2.1

Per capita income in the three income regions of the United States 1880–1959 as percentage of the per capita income of the main sequence.

Year	Far West	Main sequence	South
1880	330	100	51
1890	310	100	51
1900	294	100	52
1910	227	100	55
1920	195	100	58
1930	183	100	59
1940	178	100	59
1950	152	100	71
1956	140	100	76
1959	137	100	77

From: William Warntz, *op. cit.*, table II, p. 50.

37 Encouraged by these results Warntz ends up with a prediction for the United States and a prediction for the whole world.

The prediction for the United States is based upon fig. 2.13. The vertical axis shows what Warntz calls the South's population surplus as a fraction of the national total population. This surplus is computed as the actual population minus the population which the South should have had if the total income were unchanged and the income per capita were equal to that of the main sequence. Fig. 2.13 indicates to Warntz that the South's population surplus will disappear about the year 2000. A similar analysis based upon what Warntz calls the Far West's population deficit indicates a zero value about year 2015. This leads Warntz to the conclusion that the regional income differences in the United States may disappear about the end of the present century.

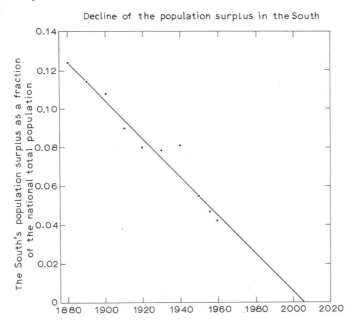

Fig. 2.13. From: William Warntz, *op. cit.*, fig. 18, p. 85.

38   The prediction for the world is not a prediction of the date when national income differences will have disappeared, but a prediction of the balance of power in a world where national per capita incomes have been equalized and where the population and its geographical distribution is equal to that of 1960.

Fig. 2.14 is in the words of Warntz "a possible expression of the distribution of world power, with its focus on China as the highest peak of World Potential, with India as an included peak within the closed contours, and with Western Europe (again with Moscow included peripherally in this mass) and the United States as separated minor order peaks" which "must be recognized as a possible geographical expression of the long-run results of the current systemic revolution. It is certainly no more inconceivable than a Roman Empire would have seemed to Pericles or a British Empire to Augustus Caesar!"[12]

39   Our conclusion is that Warntz's two books are major contributions to the theory of spatial interaction. The 1959 book is important because it calls the economist's attention to the friction of distance. The 1965 book is important because it gives the reader a better understanding of the friction of distance and because it builds this concept into an economic model in time and space.

On the other hand, it should be said that too much in the 1965 book depends upon unrealistic assumptions and wild ideas. An economist can hardly accept that the marginal productivities of migrants are zero in the states they leave and zero in the states to which they move. It is also difficult to accept that since the mineral discoveries and the Civil War, there have been no major external disturbances of the general, interregional equilibrium system of the United States, or to assume that no such disturbances will occur during the remainder of this century. Finally, it is very difficult to accept the assumptions behind the prediction of the world balance of power.

[12]William Warntz, *op. cit.*, pp. 112–113.

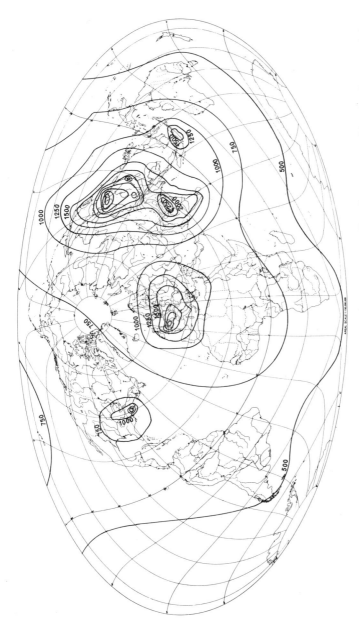

Fig. 2.14. World potential of population circa 1960, in thousands, persons per mile (all persons considered to have equal, i.e., unit weight). From: William Warntz, *op. cit.*, fig. 24, p. 111.

These deficiencies should, however, not overshadow the brilliant features of Warntz's work.

Gunnar Myrdal

40.   In a most remarkable book[13] from 1957, Gunnar Myrdal develops another theory of how trade affects factor prices.

Myrdal's approach is different from that of the Heckscher–Ohlin school. Firstly, because his analysis is a *dynamic* one whereas the Heckscher–Ohlin analysis was a static one. Secondly, because Myrdal includes *non-economic factors* in his study of what he calls the social system, whereas Heckscher and Ohlin only studied the so-called economic factors. So far, Myrdal's approach is very similar to that of the school of Social Physics. But it is different to both the Heckscher–Ohlin approach and the Social Physics approach because Myrdal finds it unrealistic to assume that there is a tendency towards automatic self-stabilization in the social system.

The Myrdal vision of the social system is that of a system always on the move. It is moved by outside pushes and pulls and by the momentum of its own internal processes. In the normal case, it moves from one disequilibrium to another and a change in the system will usually lead to supporting changes moving the system in the same direction as the first change but much further. Myrdal therefore speaks of circular causation and of the tendency of social processes to become cumulative and to gather speed at accelerating rates. Such movements can, according to Myrdal, be stopped by policy interferences or by exogenous changes working in the opposite direction of the initial change. But, left to itself, the social system will usually work as illustrated by the expressions: "Nothing succeeds like success" and "Nothing fails like failure."

[13]Gunnar Myrdal, *Economic theory and underdeveloped regions*, Duckworth & Co., London 1957.

Under these assumptions, Myrdal comes to the conclusion that a *liberalization of commodity and factor movements between nations (or regions) will probably make the rich nations (or regions) richer and the poor nations (or regions) poorer.*

41 The Myrdal theory can be illustrated by an example where the barriers to trade are removed between a rich and a poor country.

The rich country has a relatively great capital endowment and a high investment ratio. Because it has a high capital–labour ratio, the marginal productivity of labour, and thereby the wage level, is high. Because it has a great amount of capital per capita, a high property income per capita may be added to a high per capita labour income. And because it has a high per capita income, the savings ratio will be relatively high and this will pave the road for still higher income. Further, because the country is rich, it has been able to invest relatively great amounts in education, research and development. It has therefore a well-educated population and a relatively high technology. Finally, it has a large share of the labour force employed in the expanding tertiary and secondary industries and only a small percentage in agriculture and other primary production.

The poor country has a relatively small capital endowment and a low investment ratio. Because of the low capital–labour ratio, the marginal productivity of labour, and thereby the wage level, is low. And because of the small amount of capital per capita, the per capita property income may also be low. The total per capita income will therefore be low, as will the savings ratio, and progress will be slow. Further, because the country is poor, it has not been able to invest very much in education, research and development. It has therefore a relatively un-educated population and a low level of technology. Finally, the poor country employs a large share of its labour force in agriculture and other primary production and only a small percentage in the expanding secondary and tertiary industries.

The comparative advantages of the rich country are in the capital and research-intensive products of the secondary and tertiary industries. The comparative advantages of the poor country are in the labour- and land-intensive products of agriculture and other primary production. When the barriers to trade are removed, the rich country will export advanced industrial products to the poor country and the poor country will export traditional primary products to the rich country. The question is now: How will this trade affect income per capita in the two countries?

42   In the rich country, the answer is rather easy to give. The removal of barriers to trade with the poor country will give the new and expanding capital- and research-intensive industries an extra outlet for their products and this will speed up the rich country's economic development. The import-competing primary production may, however, suffer from the trade liberalization, but this will be no serious problem for the rich nation. Firstly, because it only employs a small share of the labour force in primary production. Secondly, because the country, under any circumstances and as a part of the development process, must transfer resources from primary to secondary and tertiary production. The high level of education has probably made the population aware of this and most of those employed in primary production certainly do know that, sooner or later, they may have to find another job. The liberalization of trade will only make them feel that things move a little faster than they originally thought. Finally, the transition will be facilitated by the expansion of the export industries, creating additional demand for labour and capital.

This leads to the conclusion that the liberalization of trade will probably make the rich country richer.

43   It is, however, more difficult to say how the removal of barriers to trade will affect the per capita income of the poor country.

The interaction between the two countries will in the poor country have two groups of effects which Myrdal calls "spread effects" and "backwash effects" respectively.

The *spread effects* are the effects making the poor country better off. In the case of the removal of the barriers to trade, the spread effects will be better outlets for the primary products, maybe an improvement of the terms of trade and possibly a more rapid diffusion of innovations as a result of the more intensive interaction with the rich and technically advanced country.

The *backwash effects* are the effects making the poor country worse off. In the case of the removal of barriers to trade, the backwash effects manifest themselves in the possible slow-down of the poor country's economic development. In most countries, long-run economic development is a question of moving resources out of primary production and into secondary and tertiary industries. By creating new outlets for the poor country's primary products, the liberalization of trade contributes to the maintenance of resources in the poor country's primary production. And by creating competition for the poor country's infant secondary and tertiary industries, the liberalization of trade makes it difficult for the poor country to develop these industries. If the rich country's export industries are far more competitive than the poor country's import-competing industries, the removal of barriers to trade may even destroy the poor country's new industries.

The net effect of trade liberalization on the poor country's income depends upon the balance between the spread effects and the backwash effects. If the difference in income between the two countries is rather limited, the spread effects may outweigh the backwash effects and the poor country may benefit from the trade liberalization. But the backwash effects will increase in importance with the difference between the economic development of the countries. If the difference is substantial, the backwash effects may be strong enough to slow down the poor country's development. In this case, trade liberalization may create new inequalities in the international distribution of income by speeding up economic growth in the rich country and slowing it down in the poor country. In relation to the rich country, the removal of barriers to trade will then make the poor country poorer. But if the difference in the two countries' economic development is very great, the liberalization of trade may even in absolute terms make the poor country poorer.

44   If the liberalization of trade is followed up by a liberalization of capital movements, Myrdal is afraid that capital may move from the poor country to the rich country and thus reinforce the tendencies towards a more unequal international distribution of income.

Unlike the neoclassical economists, Myrdal believes that the net return on capital may be higher in the rich than in the poor countries.

This difference of opinion can partly be explained by different assumptions about production functions. The neoclassical economists assumed identical production functions in the two countries. The law of diminishing returns would then lead to a relatively low return on capital in the rich country and a relatively high return in the poor country. Myrdal assumes a higher level of technology in the rich country. The same input of capital will *ceteris paribus* produce a greater output in the rich than in the poor country and this may outweigh the effects of the law of diminishing returns.

Myrdal further takes into account that the rich country may have a more developed money and capital market than the poor country. An asset in the rich country may therefore be more liquid than a corresponding asset in the poor country. This may also induce capitalists of the poor country to invest their capital abroad.

Finally, Myrdal emphasizes that political and economic conditions may be more stable in the rich country. This may reduce the risks of investment in the rich country compared to those in the poor country.

45 A liberalization of the international movements of labour may also make the rich countries richer and the poor countries poorer. Migration is selective, says Myrdal. It may very well be the young, well educated people who leave the poor country. This may slow down the poor country's economic development and speed up that of the rich country.

46 Summing up, we can say that Myrdal's theory is a remarkable one because it substitutes the principle of circular and cumulative causation for the principle of stable equilibrium.

It is also remarkable because it describes the effect of international and interregional trade and factor movements upon income as a net outcome of an interplay between spread effects and backwash effects.

Myrdal's own impression is that trade and factor movements may make rich nations and regions richer and poor nations and regions poorer. But he emphasizes that such an outcome becomes more probable, the farther the economic development of the nations or regions concerned are from each other. He further emphasizes that the spread effects may be stronger and the back-wash effects weaker between the regions of a rich country than between the regions of a poor country.

Myrdal gives some evidence in support of his ideas, but not very much is said about regional income differences in the United States. These differences have been subject to several empirical studies which do not support the Myrdal hypothesis.[14]

[14]See e.g. George H. Borts and Jerome L. Stein, *Economic growth in a free market*, Columbia University Press, New York and London 1964; and J. Thomas Romans, *Capital exports and growth among U.S. regions*, The New England Research Series, no. 1, Wesleyan University Press, Middletown, Conn. 1965.

The aim of this chapter has, however, not been to verify or dismiss the Myrdal conclusions, but only to present his basic thought.

Conclusions

47   The theories surveyed in this chapter all try to explain how trade and related spatial interaction affect the international (or interregional) distribution of income. As expected, they are very different in their approaches and their results. Here, we shall mention four major differences.

First, the Heckscher–Ohlin model is a conventional economic one, whereas the models in Social Physics and Gunnar Myrdal's model include non-economic explanatory variables.

Secondly, the Heckscher–Ohlin model is a static one, whereas those of the school of Social Physics and Gunnar Myrdal are dynamic ones.

Thirdly, Myrdal believes that trade and related spatial interaction may lead to an increase in national or regional income differences, whereas the Heckscher–Ohlin school and the school of Social Physics believe in a tendency towards a more equal spatial distribution of income.

Fourthly, those believing in equalization have different reasons for doing so. The Heckscher–Ohlin school believes that trade will equalize commodity prices which in turn will equalize factor prices. The school of Social Physics believes neither that trade will equalize commodity prices, nor that this by itself would lead to an equalization of factor prices. But it believes in a more equal spatial income distribution as the long-run result of a number of built-in social adjustment mechanisms.

48   In the model to be constructed in chapter 3 we shall integrate some of the basic elements of the models surveyed above.

From the Heckscher–Ohlin model we shall use the interdependence between commodity prices and factor prices.

From the models of the school of Social Physics we shall use the Warntz interpretation of the concept friction of distance. Both that it reflects that spatial adjustment processes take time and that the time needed is a function of the general level of information.

From the same group of models and from Gunnar Myrdal we shall use the dynamic set-up and a number of so-called non-economic variables, such as education, urbanization, etc.

From Gunnar Myrdal we shall further use "spread effects" and "backwash effects".

Let us now turn to chapter 3 to see how.

PART 2

Regional income differences

An economic model in time and space

1 In this chapter we shall construct an economic model in time and space determining the regional income differences in a nation. The model shall integrate basic elements of the theories surveyed in part 1. In part 3 it shall be tried against available data on the spatial economic history of the United States from 1880 to 1950.

Because we want to simplify the comparison of the values computed by the model with the historical statistics, we shall make our model a deterministic, recursive one.

Because we want to save time and money we shall make our model such that it can be operated by a high-speed electronic computer.

The analytical framework

2 Constructing and operating a comprehensive, recursive computer model is, in fact, to do a follow-up of Gunnar Myrdal's 1957 book.

Myrdal saw the economic system as part of a social system always on the move. That is what we shall do. And like Myrdal, we shall make it our main scientific task "to analyse the causal interrelations within the system itself as it moves under the influence of outside pushes and pulls and the momentum of its own internal processes".[1]

Myrdal analysed these interrelations qualitatively. But he emphasized that the ideal solution of the scientific problem was

[1]Gunnar Myrdal, *op. cit.*, p. 18.

"an interconnected set of quantitative equations, describing the movement, and the internal changes, of the system studied under the various influences which are at work". And he continued: "That this complete, quantitative and truly scientific formulation is far beyond the horizon does not need to be pointed out; but in principle it could be made, and I submit that the working out of such a complete and quantitative solution should be the aim of our research endeavours even when they have to stop far away from the ideal".[2]

Challenged by Myrdal, we shall try a follow-up profiting from recent progress in computer techniques.

3   Much could be said about recursive computer models.[3] Here it should be sufficient to mention that a recursive economic model is a model which can follow an economy's development over time, that a recursive computer model is a recursive model designed for the use of high-speed electronic computers and that the use of such computers has certain advantages.

It may be important that the use of computers makes it possible to operate rather complicated economic models. It may also be important that recently developed computer simulation techniques make it possible to find particular numerical solutions to equations in some cases where an exact analytic solution seems to be out of reach.

What counts here is, however, that a computer model can do a very good job following an economy's development over time, both in the cases where the economy moves towards an equilibrium and in the cases where the economy moves from one disequilibrium to another.

4   It may be difficult to construct and operate a recursive computer model. But in principle it is very simple.

First, a conventional economic model must be presented in the form of a set of functional relationships describing the

[2]Gunnar Myrdal, *op. cit.,* p. 19.
[3]See e.g. Thomas H. Naylor, Joseph L. Balintfy, Donald S. Burdick and Kong Chu, *Computer simulation techniques,* John Wiley, New York, London and Sidney 1966.

interaction between the variables and the components of the model.

Secondly, the conventional economic model must be made a computer model by a computer program, telling a computer how to operate the model in a sequence of runs.

Thirdly, the parameters of the model and the so-called status variables must be read into the computer. The status variables are the values of the model's variables at time *t* which is the starting point of the simulation.

Fourthly, the runs should begin. Each run has an input and an output. The status variables are input in the first run of the computer. The output shows the values of the variables at time *t* + 1. These values are used as input in the second run where the output will show the values of the variables at time *t* + 2. And so on. The principle is that the output of each run serves as input in the next run.

Finally, the results of the analysis should be tested in one way or another. This is by no means easy.[4]

The functional relationships

5   Turning to the functional relationships means turning away from Gunnar Myrdal and approaching the Heckscher–Ohlin school and the school of Social Physics.

Myrdal's principle of circular and cumulative causation states that the disequilibrating forces of the economy will far outweigh the equilibrating ones. This leads him to the conclusion that regional income differences may widen over time in an economy left to itself.

The Heckscher–Ohlin school and the school of Social Physics believe in the principle of stable equilibrium, i.e., that the equilibrating forces of the economy will far outweigh the

[4]See, e.g., Charles C. Holt, "Validation and application of macroeconomic models using computer simulation," in: James S. Duesenberry, Gary Fromm, Lawrence R. Klein and Edwin Kuh, editors, *The Brookings quarterly econometric model of the United States.* Rand McNally and North-Holland Publ. Co., Chicago and Amsterdam 1965, pp. 636–650.

disequilibrating ones. This leads the members of both schools to the conclusion that regional income differences will have a tendency to disappear over time in an economy left to itself.

We shall see regional differences in per capita income as the net result of a complicated interaction between equilibrating and disequilibrating forces.

6 Our starting point is the regional production functions:

$$Y_i^t = \gamma_i^t [\delta_i^t (K_i^t)^{-\beta_i^t} + (1 - \delta_i^t)(L_i^t)^{-\beta_i^t}]^{-1/\beta_i^t}, \qquad (3.1)$$

where Y_i^t = flow of regional income from time t to time $t+1$ in region i $(i = 1, 2, \ldots, n)$,

K_i^t = stock of capital at time t in region i,

L_i^t = stock of labour (labour force) at time t in region i, or flow of labour services per unit of time from time t to time $t+1$ in region i,

γ_i^t = efficiency parameter from time t to time $t+1$ in the aggregate CES production function of region i,

δ_i^t = distribution parameter from time t to time $t+1$ in the aggregate CES production function of region i,

β_i^t = substitution parameter from time t to time $t+1$ in the aggregate CES production function of region i.

7 The production functions expressed by equation (3.1) belong to the group of so-called "CES" or "homohypallagic" production functions. This group was introduced into the literature by Arrow, Chenery, Minhas and Solow in a most remarkable 1961 article.[5] The letters CES stand for the words

[5]Kenneth J. Arrow, Hollis B. Chenery, Bagicha S. Minhas and Robert M. Solow, "Capital-labour substitution and economic efficiency," *Review of Economics and Statistics,* vol. 43, no. 3, August 1961, pp. 225–250. The article is brilliant but difficult to read. Easier to read is the exposition presented by one of the co-authors of the 1961 article in the book: Bagicha S. Minhas, *An international comparison of factor costs and factor use,* Contributions to Economic Analysis, vol. 31, North-Holland Publ. Co., Amsterdam 1963, or Helmut Frisch, "Die CES-Funktion," *Zeitschrift für Nationalökonomie,* Band 24, Heft 4, 1964, pp. 419–444.

"constant elasticity of substitution" which was the original name of the production function. The name "homohypallagic" was used by Minhas in a later work.[6] It is compounded from two Greek words: "Homo" which means "same" and "hypallage" which means "substitution".

But why did we choose the CES production function for our model?

8   Our choice of production function was determined by three major considerations.

Firstly, we wanted to assume constant returns to scale. We therefore had to choose a production function which was homogeneous of the first degree.

Secondly, we wanted a production function which was well known in the economic literature. This limited our choice to the Leontief function. the Cobb–Douglas function or the CES function.

Thirdly, we wanted a production function which could take into account the different industrial structures of the different regions.

To show how this led us to the CES function, we shall introduce two well-known concepts: the marginal rate of substitution between the factors of production, called R, and the elasticity of substitution between the factors of production, called σ.

9   Fig. 3.1 is an ordinary isoquant map. Assuming constant returns to scale, we can illustrate the production function in question by a single insoquant (Y).

The actual factor combination is indicated by the point P. The average capital–labour ratio (K/L) is equal to the slope of the dotted line OP.

---

[6]B. S. Minhas, *op. cit.*, p. 32. Here Minhas gives credit for suggesting the name to Emmanuel G. Mesthene of the Rand Corporation, Santa Monica, California.

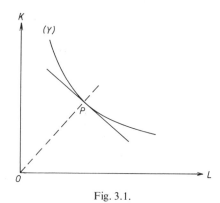

Fig. 3.1.

The marginal rate of substitution between capital and labour

$$R = -\frac{dK}{dL} \tag{3.2}$$

is the numerical value of the slope of the (fully drawn) tangent to the isoquant at P.

The elasticity of substitution between the factors of production

$$\sigma = \frac{d(K/L)/(K/L)}{dR/R} \tag{3.3}$$

measures the relative change in the slope of OP in terms of the relative change in the slope of the tangent as P moves along the isoquant.

The elasticity of substitution therefore tells us something about the shape of the isoquant, i.e., the properties of the production function.

The elasticity of substitution may change as P moves along the isoquant. But in special cases it may remain constant. The production function is then called a CES production function and it is described by a formula like equation (3.1) where

$$\beta = \frac{1}{\sigma} - 1. \tag{3.4}$$

10 Such special cases are those represented by the Leontief function and the Cobb–Douglas function.[7] The Leontief function is a CES function where $\sigma = 0$ and the Cobb–Douglas function is a CES function where $\sigma = 1$.

We may therefore ask whether we could expect σ to be either 0 or 1. The answer is: probably not. In an international study of 24 industries, B. S. Minhas has shown that for most industries the elasticity of substitution differs significantly from both zero and unity.[8]

This could be reason enough for choosing the CES function instead of one of the two other production functions.

11 Our main reason is, however, that the elasticity of substitution seems to vary considerably between industries.[9]

We know that the regions we are going to study have different industrial structures. We must therefore expect that they also have different elasticities of substitution in their aggregate regional production functions. This can be taken into account by using CES functions; cf. eq. (3.1) where the subscript i indicates that β may vary from region to region.

12 The regional production functions (3.1) determine regional production or regional income at time t as a function of the values at time t of certain parameters and variables.

The basic idea of a recursive model is that the values at time $t+1$ of certain parameters and variables are determined by values at time t. So our next task is to specify how the values at time $t+1$ of the regional capital stocks, labour forces, efficiency parameters, substitution parameters and distribution parameters are determined by values at time t.

[7]Formal proof can be found in Arrow, Chenery, Minhas and Solow, *op. cit.*, but it may be easier to read Roy G. D. Allen, *Macro-economic theory*, Macmillan, London and New York 1967, pp. 51–55.

[8]B. S. Minhas, *op. cit.*, pp. 21–26.

[9]See Arrow, Chenery, Minhas and Solow, *op. cit.*, p. 240, and B. S. Minhas, *op. cit.*, p. 20.

Such information would enable us to compute the values at time $t+1$ of regional incomes.

13 We shall determine the capital stock at time $t+1$ in region i as:

$$K_i^{t+1} = K_i^t \, e^\Gamma \left(\frac{y_i^t}{y^t}\right)^\zeta \left(\frac{r_i^t}{r^t}\right)^\eta \left(\frac{_iV^t}{V^t}\right)^\vartheta;$$ (3.5)

where:

$$y_i^t = \frac{Y_i^t}{P_i^t};$$ (3.6)

$$P_i^t = aL_i^t;$$ (3.7)

$$y^t = \frac{\sum_{i=1}^n Y_i^t}{\sum_{i=1}^n P_i^t};$$ (3.8)

$$r^t = \frac{\sum_{i=1}^n r_i^t K_i^t}{\sum_{i=t}^n K_i^t};$$ (3.9)

$$_iV^t = \sum_{j=1}^n \frac{y_j^t P_j^t}{d_{ij}} = \sum_{j=1}^n \frac{Y_j^t}{d_{ij}};$$ (3.10)

$$V^t = \frac{\sum_{i=1}^n {}_iV^t}{n};$$ (3.11)

where y_i^t = flow of regional income from time t to time $t+1$ in region i per inhabitant at time t in region i ($i = 1, 2, \ldots, n$),

y^t = flow of national income from time t to time $t+1$ per inhabitant at time t in the nation,

P_i^t = stock of inhabitants (population) at time t in region i,

r_i^t = flow of return on capital from time t to time $t+1$ in region i per unit of capital at time t in region i,

$r^t =$ flow of return on capital from time t to time $t+1$ in the nation per unit of capital at time t in the nation,

$_iV^t =$ gross economic population potential at time t in region i,

$V^t =$ the average of the nation's n regional gross economic population potentials at time t,

$d_{ij} =$ the distance between region i and region j ($i = 1$, $2, \ldots, n$), ($j = 1, 2, \ldots, n$),

$e =$ the base of the natural logarithm.

$(\Gamma > 0, \zeta > 0, \eta > 0, \vartheta > 0,$ constants$).$ $(a > 1,$ constant$.)$

Eq. (3.5) thus determines the stock of capital in a region at time $t+1$ as a function of the region's capital stock at time t (the first factor), the rate of growth in the nation's capital stock (the second factor), the region's own savings (the third factor), and the capital movements (the fourth and the fifth factor).

14 We might now ask: what is the theory behind eq. (3.5)? Let us start by admitting that two assumptions are made for convenience. Firstly, that the function is linear in the logs. Secondly, that Γ, the rate of growth per unit of time in the nation's capital stock, is constant during the period considered. We shall, however, not discuss these two assumptions. Our main concern is the differences in regional growth rates. Therefore, we shall devote our attention to the third, fourth and fifth factors on the right-hand side of eq. (3.5).

The third factor:

$$\left(\frac{y_i^t}{y^t}\right)^\zeta$$

tells us that the regional capital stock will grow relatively faster in the regions with the highest per capita incomes. Behind the assumption is the well-known economic theory of an increasing propensity to save.

The fourth factor:

$$\left(\frac{r_i^t}{r^t}\right)^\eta$$

tells us that the regional capital stock will grow relatively faster in the regions with the highest rates of return on capital. Behind this assumption is the theory that capital will move from regions with low rates of return to regions with high rates of return.

The fifth factor:

$$\left(\frac{_iV^t}{V^t}\right)^\vartheta$$

gives the relation between the region's gross economic population potential and the national average of regional gross economic population potentials. This relation is an index of the relative level of interaction between the region and the rest of the nation. The fifth factor on the right-hand side of eq. (3.5) is a corollary to the fourth. It tells us that the speed of the capital movements in and out of a region will vary directly with the region's relative level of interaction with the rest of the nation. Behind this assumption is the theory that the knowledge about the rate of return to capital outside the region will be best in the regions with the most intensive interaction with other regions.

15   The labour force at time $t+1$ in region i is determined as:

$$L_i^{t+1} = L_i^t \, e^\Theta \left(\frac{y^t}{y_i^t}\right)^H \left(\frac{w_i^t}{w^t}\right)^\lambda \left(\frac{_iV^t}{V^t}\right)^\mu ; \tag{3.12}$$

where:

$$w^t = \frac{\sum_{i=1}^n w_i^t L_i^t}{\sum_{i=1}^n L_i^t} ; \tag{3.13}$$

where w_i^t = flow of wage payments from time t to time $t+1$ in region i per labour at time t in region i ($i = 1, 2, \ldots, n$),

w^t = flow of wage payments from time t to time $t+1$ in the nation per labour at time t in the nation.

($\Theta > 0$, H > 0, $\lambda > 0$, $\mu > 0$, constants).

Eq. (3.12) thus determines the labour force at time $t+1$ in region i as a function of the region's labour force at time t (the first factor), the rate of growth in the nation's labour force (the second factor), the natural increase in the labour force (the third factor), and the labour movements (the fourth and the fifth factor).

16 In presenting the theory behind eq. (3.12) we shall discuss only the assumptions behind the third, fourth and fifth factor on the right-hand side.

The third factor:

$$\left(\frac{y^t}{y_i^t}\right)^H$$

tells us that the labour force will grow relatively faster in the poor regions. Behind this assumption is the theory that the birth rate varies inversely with per capita income. The natural rate of growth of the labour force should therefore be highest in the poor regions.

The fourth and the fifth factor:

$$\left(\frac{w_i^t}{w^t}\right)^\lambda \quad \text{and} \quad \left(\frac{_iV^t}{_iV}\right)^\mu$$

reflect the theory that labour will move from low-wage to high-wage regions and that the speed of the movements in and out of a region will be highest for the regions with the most intensive interaction with the rest of the nation.

Before we leave the theories behind the determination of regional labour forces, we ought to mention that we have assumed away all difficulties arising from different rates of growth in population and labour force; cf. eq. (3.7).

17 Eq. (3.14) determines the efficiency parameter from time $t+1$ to time $t+2$ in the CES production function of region i as:

$$\gamma_i^{t+1} = \gamma_i^t \, e^{\Lambda} \left(\frac{E_i^t}{E^t}\right)^{\nu} \left(\frac{U_i^t}{U^t}\right)^{\pi} \left(\frac{_iV^t}{V^t}\right)^{\tau};$$
(3.14)

where:

$$E^t = \frac{\sum_{i=1}^{n} E_i^t L_i^t}{\sum_{i=1}^{n} L_i^t};$$
(3.15)

$$U^t = \frac{\sum_{i=1}^{n} U_i^t P_i^t}{\sum_{i=1}^{n} P_i^t};$$
(3.16)

where E_i^t = average number of years of school completed by the labour force at time t in region i ($i = 1, 2, \ldots, n$),

E^t = average number of years of school completed by the labour force at time t in the nation,

U_i^t = the percentage of the population at time t in region i living in urban communities with more than a given number of inhabitants,

U^t = the percentage of the population at time t in the nation living in urban communities with more than a given number of inhabitants.

$(\Lambda > 0, \nu > 0, \pi > 0, \tau > 0$, constants).

Eq. (3.14) thus determines the efficiency parameter from time $t+1$ to time $t+2$ in the CES production function of region i as a function of the regional efficiency parameter from t to time $t+1$ (the first factor), the national over-all *increase in*

productivity (the second factor) and different factors of importance for the inventive activity and the diffusion of innovations
(the third, the fourth and the fifth factor).

18 The theory behind the third, fourth and fifth factor on the
right side of eq. (3.14) is that the increase in productivity will
be relatively stronger in the regions where the population is
best educated, most urbanized and in closest contact with the
rest of the nation. Books by Allan R. Pred[10] and Everett M.
Rogers[11] for example, present evidence for a positive correlation
between the inventive activity in a region and the region's
educational level as well as its degree of urbanization. They
also present evidence for a positive correlation between the
speed of diffusion of innovations and the region's educational
level as well as the level of its interaction with the rest of the
nation.

19 Eq. (3.14) brought into the picture two new variables. This
creates a need for two new functional relationships determining their development over time.

Eq. (3.17) determines the average number of years of school
completed by the labour force at time $t+1$ in region i as:

$$E_i^{t+1} = E_i^t e^{\Xi} \left(\frac{y_i^t}{y^t}\right)^v \left(\frac{U_i^t}{U^t}\right)^\varphi \left(\frac{{}_iV^t}{V^t}\right)^X; \tag{3.17}$$

where ($\Xi > 0, v > 0, \varphi > 0, X > 0$, constants).

Eq. (3.17) thus determines a region's level of education at
time $t+1$ as a function of its educational level at time t (the
first factor), the increase in the national level of education
(the second factor) and different factors influencing the demand

---

[10]Allan R. Pred, *The spatial dynamics of U.S. urban-industrial growth 1800–
1914*, Regional Science Studies Series, no. 6, M.I.T. Press, Cambridge, Mass.
and London 1966.
[11]Everett M. Rogers, *Diffusion of innovations*, The Free Press of Glencoe, New
York 1962.

for and the supply of education (the third, the fourth and the fifth factor).

The theory behind the third, fourth and fifth factor on the right-hand side of eq. (3.17) is that the demand for education will be relatively stronger in regions with a relatively high per capita income and that the supply of educational facilities will be relatively greater in the most urbanized regions with the highest levels of interaction with the rest of the nation.

20 Eq. (3.18) determines the percentage of the population at time $t+1$ in region i living in urban communities with more than a given number of inhabitants as:

$$U_i^{t+1} = U_i^t \, e^{\Omega} \left(\frac{y_i^t}{y^t}\right)^{\psi} \left(\frac{iV^t}{V^t}\right)^{\omega};$$

(3.18)

where $(\Omega > 0, \psi > 0, \omega > 0$, constants).

Eq. (3.18) thus determines a region's urbanization at time $t+1$ as a function of its urbanization at time t (the first factor), the increase in the urbanization of the nation (the second factor) and two factors of importance for the propensity to agglomerate (the third and the fourth factor).

The theory behind the third and fourth factor on the right-hand side of eq. (3.18) is that growth industries as a general rule are urban industries, enjoying agglomeration economies, paying high wages and making good profits. In regions where such industries are important, we should expect a relatively strong economic growth which might lead to a relatively fast increase in the level of urbanization. And in these regions we should also expect relatively high per capita incomes and relatively high gross economic population potentials.

21 For convenience, we shall assume that the regional elasticities of substitution between capital and labour are constant over time, i.e., that

$$\sigma_i^{t+1} = \sigma_i^t.$$

(3.19)

This assumption implies, cf. eq. (3.4), that

$$\beta_i^{t+1} = \beta_i^t. \tag{3.20}$$

During the whole period under consideration we shall therefore work with unchanged substitution parameters in our regional CES production functions. This may be somewhat unrealistic if the regional compositions of industries change significantly.

22 For convenience, we shall also assume that the regional distribution parameters are constant over time, i.e., that

$$\delta_i^{t+1} = \delta_i^t. \tag{3.21}$$

23 In paragraph 5 above it was said that we should see regional income differences as the net result of a complicated interaction between equilibrating and disequilibrating forces. We have now specified the functional relationships of our model. We may then ask: Which are the equilibrating forces and which are the disequilibrating ones?

The equilibrating forces can be found in the basic elements from the Heckscher–Ohlin model represented in eqs. (3.1), (3.5) and (3.12). Eq. (3.1) is a CES function belonging to the group of well-behaved production functions designed for the conventional economic general equilibrium analysis. It has constant returns to scale and decreasing marginal products of labour and capital. If a factor becomes more abundant, its marginal product declines and so does its remuneration when it is paid the value of the marginal product. The importance of this property becomes obvious when we allow for interregional factor movements as we do in eqs. (3.5) and (3.12). These two equations also have elements from the models in social physics working towards equalization via factor movements.

The disequilibrating forces can be found in eqs. (3.5), (3.12), (3.14), (3.17) and (3.18) which included basic elements from the

Myrdal theory. Eq. (3.5) tells about the tendency of capital to accumulate fastest in the rich regions and Eq. (3.12) about the tendency of the labour supply to grow fastest in the poor regions. Eqs. (3.14), (3.17) and (3.18) show how the levels of productivity, education and urbanization may increase most rapidly in the rich regions.

How to run the model

24 The program telling a computer how to operate our model could be written on the basis of the flow chart of fig. 3.2.

Block 1 in the flow chart specifies the parameters and the status variables which should be read into the computer as input data. The first line brings the numbers of regions, the regional substitution parameters and the regional distribution parameters, cf. eqs. (3.1), (3.20) and (3.21). The next seven lines specify the parameters of eqs. (3.5), (3.7), (3.10), (3.12), (3.14), (3.17) and (3.18) respectively.

The status variables are specified in the last two lines of block 1. First, the values from time 0 to time 1 of the total regional incomes, the per capita regional incomes and the efficiency parameters in the regional production functions. Then, the values at time 0 of the regional capital stocks, the regional labour forces, the regional levels of education and the regional degrees of urbanization.

25 Block 2 sets t equal to zero. The variables specified in block 3 should therefore be computed for $t = 0$.

The first line in block 3 specifies variables from eq. (3.5). The values of y_i^0/y^0 are computed from the status variables Y_i^0 and L_i^0 and eqs. (3.6), (3.7) and (3.8). The values of r_i^0/r^0 are computed from the status variables Y_i^0, γ_i^0, K_i^0 and L_i^0 and eqs. (3.1) and (3.9). The values of $_iV^0/V^0$ are computed from the status variables Y_i^0 and eqs. (3.10) and (3.11).

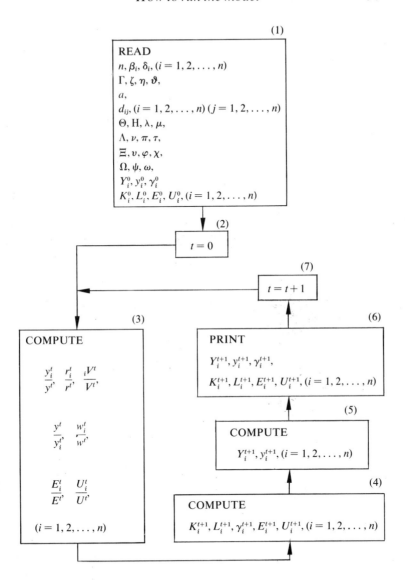

Fig. 3.2.

The second line in block 3 specifies variables from eq. (3.12). The values of y^0/y_i^0 are computed in the same way as the values of y_i^0/y^0. The values of w_i^0/w^0 are computed from the status variables Y_i^0, γ_i^0, K_i^0 and L_i^0 and eqs. (3.1) and (3.13).

The third line in block 3 specifies variables from eq. (3.14). The values of E_i^0/E^0 are computed from the status variables E_i^0 and L_i^0 and eq. (3.15). The values of U_i^0/U^0 are computed from the status variables U_i^0 and L_i^0 and eqs. (3.7) and (3.16).

26 The variables enumerated in block 4 are the dependent variables of eqs. (3.5), (3.12), (3.14), (3.17) and (3.18), respectively. Their values are computed from the status variables K_i^0, L_i^0, γ_i^0, E_i^0 and U_i^0 and the values of the variables specified in block 3.

The values of the variables specified in block 5 are computed from the values of the first three variables (K_i^1, L_i^1 and γ_i^1) of block 4 and eqs. (3.1) and (3.7).

27 Block 6 demands that the computer should print the values of Y_i^1, y_i^1, γ_i^1, K_i^1, L_i^1, E_i^1 and U_i^1.

When this is done, we are ready for a new run of the computer. Block 7 therefore demands that the value of t should be increased by 1 unit of time and an arrow brings us back to block 3.

And so on.

Conclusions

28 We have constructed a recursive computer model which integrates basic elements of the most important theories of interregional and international trade and related spatial interaction. Nothing has been included which is not supported by evidence in the literature but, in between, we have made some rather heroic abstractions.

The problem now is whether the model makes sense at all. We shall try to answer this question in part three of the book.

PART 3

United States 1880–1950

CHAPTER 4

The method to be used

1 In this part of the book we shall try our model against available data on the spatial history of the American economy from 1880 to 1950.

Had annual data been available for all the variables in which we are interested, we should have estimated the parameters of our model in a fullfledged econometric analysis. Together with the values of the status variables, these estimates should have been read into a computer and we should have started running the model. This would have given us the relevant series of computed values of the variables which should be compared with the observed values.

2 Even such a test of the model would have been more than difficult. The theory of how to test models like ours is only in its beginning, cf. chapter 3, paragraph 4 above.

Our problem is, however, that we do not have data enough for reliable estimates of the parameters. This leads us to a choice between two possibilities.

One is trying to get the desired data. This solution was given up. Firstly, because the author is a non-American. He knows too little about how figures are produced in America to embark upon such a project. Secondly, because the project would certainly not be a one man's job. And our resources are more than limited. Thirdly, because the relevance of the model should be shown before we invest in tailor-made data. This had not been done.

3 The other possibility is to lower our level of ambition, giving up the econometric analysis and the formal test of the model.

This possibility was chosen but it does not mean that everything is given up.

We admit that we can not test the model. But we can use the available data to get an impression of whether the model makes sense at all.

We also admit that we can not estimate the parameters of the model in an ordinary econometric analysis. But we can use the available data to get an impression of the orders of magnitude of the parameters.

4 In chapter 5 we shall present and organize the data to be used. In chapter 6 we shall produce some very preliminary "estimates" of the parameters. What is done looks like unqualified statistics or econometrics. But we do not take it for more than a hint about the order of magnitude of the parameters. In chapters 7 and 8 the "estimates" shall be used running the model under different assumptions. In chapter 9 the "estimates" of chapter 6 are more or less given up. Instead, we shall be running the model using parameter values produced by what might be called qualified guessing. Chapter 10 gives our conclusions.

CHAPTER 5

The data to be used

The regions

1   Our first problem was how to group the states into regions. We knew that this could be done in many different ways dependent upon the purpose which the analysis should serve. We decided, however, not to be pioneers but to choose a regional grouping used in one of the successful studies of regional income differences. Our final choice was between the eight regions used in the book by Perloff and associates[1] and the nine regions used by Lee et al.[2] We ended up by choosing the nine regions, predominantly because we get most of our data from the study of population redistribution and economic growth. So it was most convenient to use the same regions as this study.

2   We thus use the following regions:

1. *New England:*	2. *Middle Atlantic:*
Main	New York
New Hampshire	New Jersey
Vermont	Pennsylvania
Massachusetts	Delaware
Rhode Island	Maryland
Connecticut	District of Columbia

[1]Harvey S. Perloff, Edgar S. Dunn, jr., Eric E. Lampard and Richard F. Muth, *Regions, resources and economic growth,* Resources for the future, Johns Hopkins Press, Baltimore 1960, pp. 6–8.
[2]Everett S. Lee, Ann Ratner Miller, Carol P. Brainerd and Richard A. Easterlin, *Population redistribution and economic growth, United States 1870–1950,* vol. 1, Methodological Considerations and Reference Tables, Prepared under the Direction of Simon Kuznets and Dorothy Swaine Thomas, American Philosophical Society, Philadelphia, Penn. 1957. See especially pp. 749–750.

3. *East North Central:*   7. *West South Central:*

Ohio	Arkansas
Indiana	Louisiana
Illinois	Oklahoma
Michigan	Texas
Wisconsin	

4. *West North Central:*   8. *Mountain:*

Minnesota	Montana
Iowa	Idaho
Missouri	Wyoming
North Dakota	Colorado
South Dakota	New Mexico
Nebraska	Arizona
Kansas	Utah
	Nevada

5. *South Atlantic:*   9. *Pacific:*

Virginia	Washington
West Virginia	Oregon
North Carolina	California
South Carolina	
Georgia	
Florida	

6. *East South Central:*

Kentucky
Tennessee
Alabama
Mississippi

3   We had a problem with the District of Columbia. It was not possible to get all the data we needed, e.g. data on income and the stock of capital. So, we decided to exclude the District of Columbia from our analysis.

The regional incomes

4 The keystone of our model is a production function. Therefore, our income concept should be the concept of regional product. Unfortunately, the data are not available.

Instead of the regional products we shall use Easterlin's data for personal income. Easterlin's concept of personal income[3] is that of the Department of Commerce, namely, "the current income received by persons from all sources, inclusive of transfers from governments and business but exclusive of transfers among persons". Easterlin subdivides personal income into three categories: service income, property income and "other" income.

"Service income" is the sum of wages and salaries (excluding employee contributions to social insurance and "other labour income" such as cash sickness compensation, etc.) and proprietors' income, with imputed rents of farm dwellings included in the agricultural components of service income.

Property income is the sum of rental income (including imputed rents of owner occupied nonfarm dwellings), personal interest income, and dividends.

"Other" income includes government and business transfer payments and "other labour income".[4]

Since our model is based upon regional production functions, we shall exclude from the analysis the category "other income" consisting chiefly of government and business transfer payments. Thus, the income concept to be used here covers only personal service income and personal property income.

5 The personal service incomes for the years 1880, 1900, 1919–21 (annual average) and 1949–51 (annual average) are given in column 1 of table 5.1. This column indicates the service incomes originating in the different regions, i.e. the payments for services rendered within the areas of the said regions.

[3]Lee, Miller, Brainerd and Easterlin, *op. cit.*, vol. 1, p. 703.
[4]*Ibid.*

TABLE 5.1

Service income, property income and total personal income 1880, 1900, 1919–21 (average) and 1949–51 (average).

	Service income (1)	Property income (2)	Total personal income (3)	Adjusted property income (4)	Adjusted total personal income (5)	Adjusted total personal income (6)
	Current dollars (millions)	Current dollars (millions)	Current dollars (millions)	Current dollars (millions)	Current dollars (millions)	1929 dollars (millions)
0. United States[a]						
1880	7,373	1,370	8,743	1,357	8,730	15,076
1900	12,868	2,522	15,390	2,476	15,344	31,251
1919–21	56,111	13,166	69,277	12,930	69,041	61,098
1949–51	179,371	23,799	203,170	–	–	134,460
1. New England						
1880	806	182	988	175	981	1,694
1900	1,245	274	1,519	244	1,489	3,033
1919–21	4,721	1,341	6,062	1,113	5,834	5,163
1949–51	11,612	1,992	13,604	–	–	9,003
2. Middle Atlantic[a]						
1880	2,307	543	2,850	478	2,785	4,810
1900	3,753	986	4,739	828	4,581	9,330

1919–21	16,254	4,674	20,928	3,786	20,040	17,735
1949–51	45,893	7,019	52,912	–	–	35,018
3. East North Central						
1880	1,699	297	1,996	315	2,014	3,478
1900	2,930	525	3,455	551	3,481	7,090
1919–21	12,658	2,734	15,392	2,898	15,556	13,766
1949–51	41,694	5,208	46,902	–	–	31,040
4. West North Central						
1880	847	121	968	143	990	1,710
1900	1,777	265	2,042	326	2,103	4,283
1919–21	5,890	1,220	7,110	1,586	7,476	6,616
1949–51	16,191	1,964	18,155	–	–	12,015
5. South Atlantic						
1880	435	68	503	73	508	877
1900	710	93	803	110	820	1,670
1919–21	3,986	636	4,622	871	4,857	4,298
1949–51	15,179	1,702	16,881	–	–	11,172
6. East South Central						
1880	440	60	500	64	504	870
1900	672	80	752	91	763	1,554
1919–21	2,683	366	3,049	483	3,166	2,802
1949–51	8,357	800	9,157	–	–	6,060
7. West South Central						
1880	313	38	351	41	354	611
1900	698	109	807	114	812	1,654
1919–21	4,048	832	4,880	790	4,838	4,281
1949–51	14,089	1,592	15,681	–	–	10,378

TABLE 5.1 (*continued*)

	Service income (1) Current dollars (millions)	Property income (2) Current dollars (millions)	Total personal income (3) Current dollars (millions)	Adjusted property income (4) Current dollars (millions)	Adjusted total personal income (5) Current dollars (millions)	Adjusted total personal income (6) 1929 dollars (millions)
8. Mountain						
1880	180	11	191	19	199	344
1900	424	49	473	79	503	1,024
1919–21	1,880	307	2,187	442	2,322	2,055
1949–51	5,808	698	6,506	–	–	4,306
9. Pacific						
1880	346	50	396	49	395	682
1900	659	141	800	133	792	1,613
1919–21	3,991	1,056	5,047	961	4,952	4,382
1949–51	20,548	2,824	23,372	–	–	15,468

[a]Excluding District of Columbia. The US figures are the sums of the regional incomes recorded in the same columns.

Sources:

(1) and (2): Lee, Miller, Brainerd and Easterlin, *op. cit.*, vol. 1, tables Y-2 and Y-5, pp. 754 and 757.

(3): Sum of (1) and (2).

(4): Table 5.2 column (5).

(5): Sum of (1) and (4).

(6): For 1880, 1900 and 1919–21: column (5) deflated by price indices 57.9, 49.1 and 113.0 (1929 = 100). For 1949–51: column (3) deflated by price index 151.1 (1929 = 100). The price indices are those presented in Lee, Miller, Brainerd and Easterlin, *op. cit.*, vol. 2, p. 144.

Column 2 of table 5.1 shows Easterlin's data for the regional property income. The data show the property incomes received by the residents of the different areas. Again, we are working with production functions. Therefore, we are more interested in figures for the property income originating in the different regions.

Some very crude estimates could be made using the information of columns (1) and (2) of table 5.2. Column (1) gives the regional distribution of wealth by location, column (2) the regional distribution of wealth by ownership. Column (3) shows column (1) as percent of column (2). Column (4) gives the Easterlin data for property income received by the residents of the different regions in 1880, 1900 and 1919–21 (annual average), i.e. the years for which Easterlin has data for wealth. The estimates of property income originating in the different regions are made by multiplying columns (3) and (4). They are given in column (5) of table 5.2 under the heading "Adjusted property income" and transferred to column (4) of table 5.1.

Returning to table 5.1, we note that column (3) gives the sums of the Easterlin data for service incomes originating in the different regions and the property incomes received by the residents of these regions. We also note that column (5) gives the sums of the service incomes and the adjusted property incomes. We further note that column (3) gives data for 4 years (1880, 1900, 1919–21 [annual average] and 1949–51 [annual average]) while column (5) only gives data for 3 of these years.

6   Up to now we have brought our data in millions of current dollars. We want, however, to exclude changes in the price level from our analysis. Column (6) of table 5.1 shows the (adjusted) personal incomes in millions of 1929 dollars. The price index used to deflate the money income data was computed by Simon Kuznets[5] from unpublished annual estimates by the National Bureau of Economic Research of net national

[5]See Lee, Miller, Brainerd and Easterlin, *op. cit.,* vol. 2 (by Kuznets, Miller and Easterlin), 1960, pp. 143–144.

TABLE 5.2
Total wealth by ownership and location, property income and adjusted property
income 1880, 1900 and 1919–21 (average).

| | Total wealth | | | Pro- | Adjusted |
	By loca-tion (1)	By owner-ship (2)	(1) As percent of (2) (3)	perty income (4)	property income (5)
				Current dollars (millions)	Current dollars (millions)
	%	%	%		
0. United States[a]					
1880	100.00	100.00	100	1,370	1,357
1990	100.00	100.00	100	2,522	2,476
1919–21	100.00	100.00	100	13,166	12,930
1. New England					
1880	11.47	11.94	96	182	175
1900	8.85	9.95	89	274	244
1919–21	7.80	9.41	83	1,341	1,113
2. Middle Atlantic[a]					
1880	31.15	35.59	88	543	478
1900	29.76	35.27	84	986	828
1919–21	26.29	32.53	81	4,674	3,786
3. East North Central					
1880	24.98	23.56	106	297	315
1900	22.46	21.29	105	525	551
1919–21	21.98	20.67	106	2,734	2,898
4. West North Central					
1880	12.29	10.40	118	121	143
1900	15.76	12.86	123	265	326
1919–21	14.71	11.32	130	1,220	1,586
5. South Atlantic					
1880	5.92	5.52	107	68	73
1900	4.82	4.08	118	93	110
1919–21	7.29	5.32	137	636	871

[a]Excluding District of Columbia. The US figures in columns (4) and (5) are the
sums of the regional property incomes recorded in these columns.

The data to be used

TABLE 5.2 *(continued)*

	Total wealth			Pro-perty income (4)	Adjusted property income (5)
	By loca-tion (1)	By owner-ship (2)	(1) As percent of (2) (3)		
	%	%	%	Current dollars (millions)	Current dollars (millions)
6. East South Central					
1880	5.51	5.18	106	60	64
1900	4.17	3.67	114	80	91
1919–21	4.15	3.15	132	366	483
7. West South Central					
1880	3.44	3.21	107	38	41
1900	5.20	4.95	105	109	114
1919–21	6.35	6.65	95	832	790
8. Mountain					
1880	1.65	0.93	177	11	19
1900	3.71	2.31	161	49	79
1919–21	3.89	2.70	144	307	442
9. Pacific					
1880	3.59	3.69	97	50	49
1900	5.28	5.61	94	141	133
1919–21	7.53	8.24	91	1,056	961

Sources:
(1) and (2): Lee, Miller, Brainerd and Easterlin, *op. cit.*, vol. 1, table 4.6, pp. 729–733.
(4): Lee, Miller, Brainerd and Easterlin, *op. cit.*, vol. 1, table Y-5, p. 757.
(5): Product of (3) and (4).

product in current and constant dollars for the United States as a whole. It is as follows (1929 = 100):

1879–1881	57.9
1899–1901	49.1
1919–1921	113.0
1949–1951	151.1

The column (6) figures for 1880, 1900 and 1919–21 give the deflated column (5) figures for the adjusted personal incomes, i.e. the sums of the service incomes and the property incomes originating in the different regions.

The column (6) figures of table 5.1 for 1949–51 give the deflated column (3) figures for personal incomes, i.e. the sums of the service incomes originating in and the property incomes received by the residents of the different regions. These un-adjusted personal income data are not so good for our purpose as the adjusted ones. But they are better than no personal income data at all.

The regional capital stocks and the regional rates of return on capital

7   Column (3) of table 5.3 gives in millions of 1929-dollars the Easterlin data for wealth by location. Column (2) gives for the years 1880, 1900 and 1919–21 (annual average) the estimates of the property incomes originating in the different regions, also in millions of 1929 dollars. The rate of return on capital given in column (4) has been computed as column (2) in percent of column (3).

The regional labour forces and the regional service incomes per labour.

8   Column (3) of table 5.4 gives the data for the regional labour forces. Column (2) gives in millions of 1929 dollars the service incomes originating in the different regions. The service incomes per labour, shown in column (4), is computed straightforward.

The regional populations

9   Table 5.5 gives the data for the regional distribution of the US population 1870–1950. The labour force participation rates are given in table 5.6. We shall, however, use the same labour

TABLE 5.3

Property income, wealth and rate of return on wealth 1880, 1900, 1919–21 (average) and 1949–51 (average).

	Adjusted property income		Wealth	Rate of return on wealth
	(1)	(2)	(3)	(4)
	Current dollars (millions)	1929 dollars (millions)	1929 dollars (millions)	%
0. United States[a]				
1880	1,357	2,345	75,030	3.13
1900	2,476	5,042	178,406	2.83
1919–21	12,930	11,442	276,983	4.13
1949–51	23,799	15,750	–	–
1. New England				
1880	175	302	8,606	3.51
1900	244	497	15,787	3.15
1919–21	1,113	985	21,607	4.56
1949–51	1,992	1,318	–	–
2. Middle Atlantic[a]				
1880	478	826	23,372	3.53
1900	828	1,686	53,089	3.18
1919–21	3,786	3,350	72,826	4.60
1949–51	7,019	4,645	–	–
3. East North Central				
1880	315	544	18,742	2.90
1900	551	1,122	40,066	2.80
1919–21	2,898	2,565	60,887	4.21
1949–51	5,208	3,447	–	–
4. West North Central				
1880	143	247	9,221	2.68
1900	326	664	28,114	2.36
1919–21	1,586	1,404	40,748	3.45
1949–51	1,964	1,300	–	–
5. South Atlantic				
1880	73	126	4,442	2.84
1900	110	224	8,598	2.61

[a]Excluding District of Columbia. The US figures in columns (1), (2) and (3) are the sums of the regional figures recorded in these columns.

TABLE 5.3 (*continued*)

	Adjusted property income		Wealth	Rate of return on wealth
	(1)	(2)	(3)	(4)
	Current dollars (millions)	1929 dollars (millions)	1929 dollars (millions)	%
5. South Atlantic				
1919–21	871	771	20,194	3.82
1949–51	1,702	1,126	–	–
6. East South Central				
1880	64	111	4,134	2.69
1900	91	185	7,439	2.49
1919–21	483	427	11,496	3.71
1949–51	800	529	–	–
7. West South Central				
1880	41	71	2,581	2.75
1900	114	232	9,276	2.50
1919–21	790	699	17,590	3.97
1949–51	1,592	1,054	–	–
8. Mountain				
1880	19	33	1,238	2.67
1900	79	161	6,618	2.43
1919–21	442	391	10,776	3.63
1949–51	698	462	–	–
9. Pacific				
1880	49	85	2,694	3.16
1900	133	271	9,419	2.88
1919–21	961	850	20,859	4.07
1949–51	2,824	1,869	–	–

Sources:
(1): For 1880, 1900 and 1919–21: table 5.2, column (5), adjusted property income. For 1949–51: table 5.1, column (2), property income.
(2): Deflation by indices described in sources to table 5.1, column (6).
(3): Lee, Miller, Brainerd and Easterlin, *op. cit.,* vol. 1, table 4.6, pp. 729–733. The figures in current dollars for total wealth by location have been deflated by indices described in sources to table 5.1, column (6).
(4): Column (2) as percent of column (3).

TABLE 5.4

Service income, labour force and service income per labour 1880, 1900, 1919–21 (average) and 1949–51 (average).

| | Service income | | Labour force | Service income per labour |
	(1)	(2)	(3)	(4)
	Current dollars (millions)	1929 dollars (millions)	Thousands	1929 dollars
0. United States[a]				
1880	7,373	12,734	17,323	735
1900	12,868	26,209	28,954	905
1919–21	56,111	49,655	41,360	1,201
1949–51	179,371	118,711	59,839	1,984
1. New England				
1880	806	1,392	1,571	886
1900	1,245	2,536	2,375	1,068
1919–21	4,721	4,178	3,229	1,294
1949–51	11,612	7,685	3,892	1,975
2. Middle Atlantic[a]				
1880	2,307	3,984	4,117	968
1900	3,753	7,644	6,736	1,135
1919–21	16,254	14,384	9,933	1,448
1949–51	45,893	30,373	13,744	2,210
3. East North Central				
1880	1,699	2,934	3,616	811
1900	2,930	5,967	5,890	1,013
1919–21	12,658	11,202	8,510	1,316
1949–51	41,694	27,594	12,461	2,214
4. West North Central				
1880	847	1,463	2,009	728
1900	1,777	3,619	3,698	979
1919–21	5,890	5,212	4,590	1,136
1949–51	16,191	10,715	5,556	1,929

[a]Excluding District of Columbia. The US figures in columns (1), (2) and (3) are the sums of the regional figures recorded in these columns.

TABLE 5.4 (*continued*)

	Service income (1)	(2)	Labour force (3)	Service income per labour (4)
	Current dollars (millions)	1929 dollars (millions)	Thousands	1929 dollars
5. South Atlantic				
1880	435	751	2,231	337
1900	710	1,446	3,341	433
1919–21	3,986	3,527	4,407	800
1949–51	15,179	10,046	6,797	1,478
6. East South Central				
1880	440	760	1,877	405
1900	672	1,369	2,890	474
1919–21	2,683	2,374	3,308	718
1949–51	8,357	5,531	4,103	1,348
7. West South Central				
1880	313	541	1,146	472
1900	698	1,422	2,320	613
1919–21	4,048	3,582	3,716	964
1949–51	14,089	9,324	5,387	1,731
8. Mountain				
1800	180	311	283	1,099
1900	424	864	663	1,303
1919–21	1,880	1,664	1,253	1,328
1949–51	5,808	3,844	1,898	2,025
9. Pacific				
1880	346	598	473	1,264
1900	659	1,342	1,041	1,289
1919–21	3,991	3,532	2,414	1,463
1949–51	20,548	13,599	6,001	2,266

Sources:
(1): Table 5.1, column (1).
(2): Deflation by indices described in sources to table 5.1, column (6).
(3): Lee, Miller, Brainerd and Easterlin, *op. cit.,* vol. 1, table L-1, p. 519, and vol. 2, table A 2.3, p. 81 (figures for 1880, 1900, 1920 and 1950).
(4): Column (2) divided by column (3).

The data to be used

Table 5.5
Regional distribution of US population 1870–1950.

					Thousands				
	1870	1880	1890	1900	1910	1920	1930	1940	1950
0. United States[a]	38,428	49,979	62,717	75,717	91,643	105,273	122,289	131,005	149,895
1. New England	3,488	4,011	4,701	5,592	6,553	7,401	8,166	8,437	9,314
2. Middle Atlantic[a]	9,717	11,578	13,917	16,827	20,814	23,934	28,131	29,627	32,825
3. East North Central	9,125	11,207	13,478	15,986	18,251	21,476	25,297	26,626	30,399
4. West North Central	3,857	6,158	8,932	10,348	11,638	12,544	13,297	13,517	14,061
5. South Atlantic	4,816	6,338	7,417	8,792	10,366	11,880	13,437	15,072	17,719
6. East South Central	4,404	5,585	6,429	7,548	8,410	8,893	9,887	10,778	11,477
7. West South Central	2,030	3,334	4,741	6,532	8,785	10,242	12,177	13,065	14,538
8. Mountain	316	653	1,214	1,675	2,634	3,336	3,702	4,150	5,075
9. Pacific	675	1,115	1,888	2,417	4,192	5,567	8,195	9,733	14,487

[a]Excluding District of Columbia. The US figures are the sums of the regional figures recorded in the same columns.

Source: Lee, Miller, Brainerd and Easterlin, *op. cit.*, vol. 1, table P-4A, p. 349.

TABLE 5.6

Labour force participation rates, by regions, 1880, 1900, 1920 and 1950.

	1880	1900	1920	1950
	%	%	%	%
0. United States[a]	34.7	38.2	39.3	39.9
1. New England	39.2	42.5	43.6	41.8
2. Middle Atlantic[a]	35.6	40.0	41.5	41.9
3. East North Central	32.3	36.8	39.6	41.0
4. West North Central	32.6	35.7	36.6	39.5
5. South Atlantic	35.2	38.0	37.1	38.4
6. East South Central	33.6	38.3	37.2	35.7
7. West South Central	34.4	35.5	36.3	37.1
8. Mountain	43.3	39.6	37.6	37.4
9. Pacific	42.4	43.1	43.4	41.4

[a]Excluding District of Columbia.
Sources: table 5.4, column (3) and table 5.5.

force participation rate for all regions during the whole period, cf. eq. (3.7)

$$p_i^t = a \, L_i^t.$$

The average of the four US labour participation rates given in table 5.6 is 38.0% corresponding to

$$a = 2.63.$$

The regional levels of education

10 The level of education is measured by the median school years completed by persons 25 years old and over. No data for years of school completed are available before 1940. The figures given in table 5.7 for the years 1910, 1920 and 1930 have been

TABLE 5.7

Median school years completed by persons 25 years old and over.

	1910	1920	1930	1940	1950
0. United States[a]	6.7	6.9	7.3	8.5	9.4
1. New England	6.9	7.0	7.6	8.9	10.1
2. Middle Atlantic[a]	6.9	7.1	7.3	8.6	9.3
3. East North Central	6.6	6.7	7.1	8.7	9.6
4. West North Central	6.7	6.9	7.3	8.7	9.3
5. South Atlantic	6.3	6.6	7.0	7.5	8.3
6. East South Central	6.4	6.8	7.2	7.7	8.2
7. West South Central	6.1	6.6	7.2	8.1	8.8
8. Mountain	6.8	6.9	7.7	9.0	10.5
9. Pacific	6.9	7.2	8.3	9.7	11.4

[a]Excluding District of Columbia.

Sources: *US Census of Population: 1950*, vol. 2, Report P-C, 1–50.

Methods: Using populations as weights, the US figures have been computed as weighed averages of regional figures and the regional figures as weighed averages of state figures. No census data on years of school completed are available before 1940. The figures for 1910, 1920 and 1930 have been derived by retrojection by age cohorts of the 1940 census data on educational attainment. This was inspired by John K. Folger and Charles B. Nam: "Educational trends from census data", *Demography*, 1964, vol. 1, no. 1, pp. 247–257. An example from New England will show how the retrojections were made. In 1940, the median years of school completed were 8.9 for persons 25 years old and over. For persons 25 to 29 years old the figure was 11.0 and for persons 35 to 39 years old 9.4. Since those being 35 to 39 years old in 1940 were 25 to 29 years old in 1930, the 1930 estimate was made as follows:

$$8.9 \frac{9.4}{11.0} = 7.6 \text{ years of school completed.}$$

Correspondingly, the 1920 estimate was made on the basis of 1940 data for persons 45 to 54 years old and the 1910 estimate on the basis of the 1940 data for persons 55 to 64 years old.

TABLE 5.8
Regional distribution of US population in urban areas 1870–1950.

					Thousands				
	1870	1880	1890	1900	1910	1920	1930	1940	1950
0. United States[a]	9,783	13,970	21,876	29,882	41,668	53,720	68,468	73,760	88,127
1. New England	1,550	2,103	2,894	3,835	4,806	5,620	6,312	6,421	6,923
2. Middle Atlantic[a]	4,225	5,692	7,939	10,753	14,513	17,774	21,493	22,367	24,066
3. East North Central	1,972	3,080	5,112	7,220	9,620	13,050	16,795	17,444	19,983
4. West North Central	731	1,118	2,306	2,945	3,867	4,726	5,556	5,993	7,018
5. South Atlantic	394	545	931	1,277	2,006	2,909	4,113	5,039	6,773
6. East South Central	386	469	817	1,131	1,574	1,994	2,779	3,165	4,080
7. West South Central	269	418	716	1,057	1,956	2,969	4,427	5,203	7,701
8. Mountain	39	141	356	542	945	1,218	1,458	1,772	2,477
9. Pacific	217	404	805	1,122	2,381	3,460	5,535	6,356	9,106

[a]Excluding District of Columbia. The US figures are the sums of the regional figures recorded in the same columns.

Source: Lee, Miller, Brainerd and Easterlin, *op. cit.*, vol. 1, table P-4B, p. 353.

derived by retrojection by age cohorts of the 1940 census data. The footnote to table 5.7 explains how it was done.

The regional degrees of urbanization

11   The degree of urbanization is measured by the percent of the population living in urban areas. Table 5.8 gives the regional distribution of the US population in urban areas 1870–1950. Table 5.9 gives the regional degrees of urbanization during the same period of time.

The distances between regions and the gross economic population potentials

12   Table 5.10 gives the distances between the regions in hundreds of statute miles. These distances shall be used to

TABLE 5.9
Percent urban of US population, by regions, 1870–1950.

	1870 %	1880 %	1890 %	1900 %	1910 %	1920 %	1930 %	1940 %	1950 %
0. United States[a]	25.5	28.0	34.9	39.5	45.5	51.0	56.0	56.3	58.8
1. New England	44.4	52.4	61.6	68.6	73.3	75.9	77.3	76.1	74.3
2. Middle Atlantic[a]	43.5	49.2	57.0	63.9	69.7	74.3	76.4	75.5	73.3
3. East North Central	21.6	27.5	37.9	45.2	52.7	60.8	66.4	65.5	65.7
4. West North Central	19.0	18.2	25.8	28.5	33.2	37.7	41.8	44.3	49.9
5. South Atlantic	8.2	8.6	12.6	14.5	19.4	24.5	30.6	33.4	38.2
6. East South Central	8.8	8.4	12.7	15.0	18.7	22.4	28.1	29.4	35.5
7. West South Central	13.3	12.5	15.1	16.2	22.3	29.0	36.4	39.8	53.0
8. Mountain	12.3	21.6	29.3	32.4	35.9	36.5	39.4	42.7	48.8
9. Pacific	32.1	36.2	42.6	46.4	56.8	62.2	67.5	65.3	62.9

[a]Excluding District of Columbia.
Sources: Lee, Miller, Brainerd and Easterlin, *op. cit.*, vol. 1, tables P-4A and P-4B, pp. 349–353.

TABLE 5.10

Distances between regions in hundreds of statute miles.

	New England (1)	Middle Atlantic (2)	East North Central (3)	West North Central (4)	South Atlantic (5)	East South Central (6)	West South Central (7)	Mountain (8)	Pacific (9)
1. New England	1	2	7.5	11	7.5	9	14.5	21	25
2. Middle Atlantic	2	1	6	10	6	9	13	20	24
3. East North Central	7.5	6	1.5	4	5	3	7	14	18
4. West North Central	11	10	4	3.5	9	6	4	10	14
5. South Atlantic	7.5	6	5	9	2	3	10	18	23
6. East South Central	9	9	3	6	3	1.5	6.5	14.5	19.5
7. West South Central	14.5	13	7	4	10	6.5	2.5	8.5	14
8. Mountain	21	20	14	10	18	14.5	8.5	3.5	6
9. Pacific	25	24	18	14	23	19.5	14	6	3.5

Source and methods: The distances between regions, d_{ij} ($i = 1, 2, \ldots, 9$) ($j = 1, 2, \ldots, 9$) $i \neq j$, have been constructed as follows: for each of the 9 regions one state has been chosen as the "centre". The centre states are: (1) Massachusetts, (2) New Jersey, (3) Indiana, (4) Iowa, (5) South Carolina, (6) Tennessee, (7) Oklahoma, (8) Utah, (9) Oregon. The distances between regions are the distances between the centre states, cf. William Warntz, *Toward a geography of price*, University of Pennsylvania Press, Philadelphia, Penn. 1959, table VIII, pp. 58–62.

The distances between regions, d_{ij} ($i = 1, 2, \ldots, 9$) ($j = 1, 2, \ldots, 9$) $i = j$, have been constructed as follows: The distances, d_{ch} ($h = 1, 2, \ldots, m$) $c \neq h$, between the centre state, c, and the $(m-1)$ other states of the region are added up and divided by the number of states in the region.

$$d_{ij} = \frac{\sum_{h=1}^{m} d_{ch}}{m} \quad (i = j)\, (c \neq h).$$

The distances between states are those presented in William Warntz, *op. cit.*, table VIII, pp. 58–62.

TABLE 5.11
Computation of $_iV^a$ and V^a for ($t = 1880, 1900, 1919-21$ and $1949-51$).

	1880		1900		1919–21		1949–51	
	Y_i	$_iV$	Y_i	$_iV$	Y_i	$_iV$	Y_i	$_iV$
1. New England	1,694	5,018	3,033	9,655	5,163	17,920	9,003	35,445
2. Middle Atlantic	4,810	6,743	9,330	13,153	17,735	24,915	35,018	50,038
3. East North Central	3,478	4,389	7,090	9,008	13,766	17,271	31,040	37,638
4. West North Central	1,710	2,471	4,283	5,281	6,616	10,108	12,015	21,894
5. South Atlantic	877	2,751	1,670	5,499	4,298	10,948	11,172	24,135
6. East South Central	870	3,192	1,554	6,451	2,802	12,561	6,060	27,691
7. West South Central	611	1,966	1,654	4,314	4,281	8,469	10,378	18,565
8. Mountain	344	1,133	1,024	2,502	2,055	5,031	4,306	11,666
9. Pacific	682	962	1,613	2,112	4,382	4,414	15,468	11,077
	$V = 3,181$		$V = 6,442$		$V = 12,404$		$V = 26,467$	

Units: Y_i: millions of 1929 dollars. $_iV$ and V: millions of 1929 dollars per 100 statute miles.

Sources: Y_i ($i = 1, 2, ..., 9$): table 5.1, column (6). $_iV$: computed using the formula (3.10) and the data presented above and in table 5.10. V: computed using formula (3.11).

compute the gross economic population potentials, cf. eqs. (3.10) and (3.11). A special problem is the need for a figure, $d_{ij}(i = j)$, showing the "distance" between a region and itself. The footnote to table 5.10 tells how this problem was solved. Table 5.11 gives the gross economic population potentials.

CHAPTER 6

"Estimating" the parameters

1 For some of the important variables of the model we have only data for three or four of the years from 1880 to 1950. We have, e.g., only figures for the regional capital stocks in 1880, 1900 and 1920 and we have only figures for regional incomes in 1880, 1900, 1920 and 1950.

The figures for the four above-mentioned years are to different degrees influenced by business cycles and special circumstances. Working with 9 regions we get 36 observations to include in our estimation work. In cases where we only have data for three years we get 27 observations. We can therefore do something looking like an ordinary regression analysis. We should, however, not forget how few, how insufficient and how unsatisfactory our data are. We must remain fully aware that the "estimates" we can do in this chapter are not estimates like those done in ordinary statistical or econometric analyses. Only preliminary hints about the order of magnitude of the parameters can be given.

For the same reason we shall not use very sophisticated methods of estimation. It simply does not pay.

The substitution parameters

2 Starting with the production functions characterized by eq. (3.1) we shall try to estimate the β's or the substitution parameters.

The substitution parameter is defined by eq. (3.4) telling that

$$\beta = \frac{1}{\sigma} - 1,$$

where σ is the elasticity of substitution. From the article by
Arrow et al.[1] we know that in general a linear relationship
between the logarithms of Y/L (the value of the output per
labour) and w (the wage rate), i.e.

$$\log \frac{Y}{L} = \log A + \sigma \log w$$

gives a good fit. (σ is the elasticity of substitution between
capital and labour and A is a constant.)

For the United States we estimate σ on the following data:
The four Y-values from table 5.1, column (6); the four L-values
from table 5.4, column (3) and the four w-values from table
5.4, column (4).

Correspondingly, we estimate the nine regional elasticities
of substitution, σ_1 $(i = 1, 2, \ldots, 9)$.

Finally we estimate the substitution parameters β and β_i
$(i = 1, 2, \ldots, 9)$ using formula (3.4). The results are as in table
6.1.

TABLE 6.1
Preliminary estimates of the σ's and the β's.

0. United States	$\sigma = 0.957$	$\beta = 0.0454$
1. New England	$\sigma_1 = 0.959$	$\beta_1 = 0.0423$
2. Middle Atlantic	$\sigma_2 = 0.941$	$\beta_2 = 0.0625$
3. East North Central	$\sigma_3 = 0.949$	$\beta_3 = 0.0540$
4. West North Central	$\sigma_4 = 0.954$	$\beta_4 = 0.0487$
5. South Atlantic	$\sigma_5 = 0.980$	$\beta_5 = 0.0202$
6. East South Central	$\sigma_6 = 0.970$	$\beta_6 = 0.0307$
7. West South Central	$\sigma_7 = 0.988$	$\beta_7 = 0.0121$
8. Mountain	$\sigma_8 = 0.970$	$\beta_8 = 0.0313$
9. Pacific	$\sigma_9 = 0.940$	$\beta_9 = 0.0641$

When estimating the σ's in conventional linear regression analyses we got no coefficient of correlation less
than 0.98.

[1]Arrow, Chenery, Minhas and Solow, *op. cit.*, eq. (8), p. 229.

The results indicate that little was won by using CES production functions. Firstly, because regional differences in the elasticities of substitution are not what we might have expected them to be. Secondly, because all the elasticities are so close to 1 that Cobb–Douglas functions probably might have done as good a job as CES functions.

The distribution parameters

3 Having estimated the β's we shall go on trying to estimate the δ's or the distribution parameters. From the Arrow et al. article[2] we know that:

$$\frac{\delta}{1-\delta} = \left(\frac{r}{w}\right)\left(\frac{K}{L}\right)^{1+\beta}. \tag{6.2}$$

For the United States we estimate δ on the following data: The simple average of the three r-values from table 5.3, column (4); the simple average of the three corresponding w-values from table 5.4, column (4); the simple average of the three K-values from table 5.3, column (3); the simple average of the three corresponding L-values from table 5.4, column (3); and the β-value from table 6.1.

In the same way, we estimate the nine regional distribution parameters, δ_i ($i = 1, 2, \ldots, 9$). The results are shown in table 6.2.

The efficiency parameters

4 Having estimated also the δ's, we shall go on trying to estimate the γ's or the efficiency parameters for 1880, 1900 and 1919–21 (average). This shall be done on the basis of the

[2]Arrow, Chenery, Minhas and Solow, *op. cit.*, eq. (21), p. 233.

TABLE 6.2

Preliminary estimates of the δ's.

0. United States	$\delta = 0.242$
1. New England	$\delta_1 = 0.243$
2. Middle Atlantic	$\delta_2 = 0.285$
3. East North Central	$\delta_3 = 0.252$
4. West North Central	$\delta_4 = 0.259$
5. South Atlantic	$\delta_5 = 0.188$
6. East South Central	$\delta_6 = 0.169$
7. West South Central	$\delta_7 = 0.169$
8. Mountain	$\delta_8 = 0.208$
9. Pacific	$\delta_9 = 0.274$

production function (3.1) or:

$$\gamma^t = \frac{Y^t}{[\delta(K^t)^{-\beta} + (1-\delta)(L^t)^{-\beta}]^{-1/\beta}}. \tag{6.3}$$

For the United States we estimate γ^t ($t = 1880$, 1900 and 1919–21) on the following data: The Y^t-value from table 5.1, column (6); the K^t-value from table 5.3, column (3); the L^t-value from table 5.4, column (3); the β-value from table 6.1; and the δ-value from table 6.2.

In the same way, we estimate the nine regional efficiency parameters γ_i^t ($i = 1, 2, \ldots, 9$) for each of the three points of time ($t = 1880$, 1900 and 1919–21). The results are shown in table 6.3.

The parameter Γ

5   We now turn to eq. (3.5). Our first task is to try to estimate the value of the parameter Γ. This is done on the national K-values from table 5.3, column (3) and eq. (6.4):

$$e^{40\Gamma} = \frac{K^{1919\text{-}21}}{K^{1880}}, \tag{6.4}$$

TABLE 6.3

Preliminary estimates of the γ''s ($t = 1880$, 1900 and 1919–21).

	$t = 1880$	$t = 1900$	$t = 1919$–21
0. United States	$\gamma = 151$	$\gamma = 176$	$\gamma = 237$
1. New England	$\gamma_1 = 175$	$\gamma_1 = 200$	$\gamma_1 = 250$
2. Middle Atlantic	$\gamma_2 = 154$	$\gamma_2 = 172$	$\gamma_2 = 225$
3. East North Central	$\gamma_3 = 157$	$\gamma_3 = 188$	$\gamma_3 = 250$
4. West North Central	$\gamma_4 = 130$	$\gamma_4 = 161$	$\gamma_4 = 195$
5. South Atlantic	$\gamma_5 = 102$	$\gamma_5 = 125$	$\gamma_5 = 221$
6. East South Central	$\gamma_6 = 142$	$\gamma_6 = 162$	$\gamma_6 = 245$
7. West South Central	$\gamma_7 = 152$	$\gamma_7 = 185$	$\gamma_7 = 292$
8. Mountain	$\gamma_8 = 252$	$\gamma_8 = 278$	$\gamma_8 = 303$
9. Pacific	$\gamma_9 = 209$	$\gamma_9 = 207$	$\gamma_9 = 244$

which gives us the preliminary estimate:

$$\Gamma = 0.0327.$$

The parameters ζ, η and ϑ

6   Our next task is to try to estimate the parameters ζ, η and ϑ. We hope this can be done in a multiple regression analysis where eq. (6.5) is used instead of eq. (3.5).

$$K_i^{t+20} = K_i^t \, e^{20\Gamma} \left(\frac{y_i^t}{y^t}\right)^{20\zeta} \left(\frac{r_i^t}{r^t}\right)^{20\eta} \left(\frac{_iV^t}{V^t}\right)^{20\vartheta}. \tag{6.5}$$

Eq. (6.5) is given the form

$$\left(\frac{y_i^t}{y^t}\right)^{20\zeta} \left(\frac{r_i^t}{r^t}\right)^{20\eta} \left(\frac{_iV^t}{V^t}\right)^{20\vartheta} = \frac{K_i^{t+20}}{K_i^t e^{20\Gamma}}, \tag{6.6}$$

and the data to be used in the multiple regression analysis are shown in table 6.4.

TABLE 6.4

Data to be used in the estimation of ζ, η and ϑ.

$t = 1880$	$\dfrac{y_i^t}{y^t}$	$\dfrac{r_i^t}{r^t}$	$\dfrac{{}_iV^t}{V^t}$	$\dfrac{K^{t+20}}{K_i^t e^{20\Gamma}}$
	(1)	(2)	(3)	(4)
1. New England	1.239	1.121	1.577	0.9549
2. Middle Atlantic	1.343	1.128	2.120	1.1824
3. East North Central	1.106	0.927	1.380	1.1128
4. West North Central	0.978	0.856	0.777	1.5871
5. South Atlantic	0.452	0.907	0.865	1.0076
6. East South Central	0.533	0.859	1.003	0.9367
7. West South Central	0.613	0.879	0.618	1.8709
8. Mountain	1.397	0.853	0.356	2.7828
9. Pacific	1.657	1.010	0.302	1.8200

$t = 1900$				
1. New England	1.184	1.113	1.499	0.7125
2. Middle Atlantic	1.284	1.124	2.042	0.7141
3. East North Central	1.116	0.989	1.398	0.7911
4. West North Central	1.073	0.834	0.820	0.7545
5. South Atlantic	0.463	0.922	0.854	1.2226
6. East South Central	0.499	0.880	1.001	0.8045
7. West South Central	0.661	0.883	0.670	0.9871
8. Mountain	1.431	0.859	0.388	0.8476
9. Pacific	1.436	1.018	0.328	1.1528

Sources: y_i^t/y^t: computed as $(Y_i^t/L_i^t)/(Y^t/L^t)$ using data from table 5.1, column (6) and table 5.4, column (3). r_i^t/r^t: table 5.3, column (4). ${}_iV^t/V^t$: table 5.11. K_i^t: table 5.3, column (3). Γ: the estimate in paragraph 5 above.

The method is questionable because we disregard the effects of the annual changes in regional capital stocks during the twenty year period. But for our purpose it is not useless.

The results shown in table 6.5 are rather discouraging for two reasons. Firstly, because the computed t-values and the 0.54 coefficient of multiple correlation are unsatisfactory.

TABLE 6.5

Results of the first multiple regression analysis.

	20ζ	20η	20ϑ
Independent variable	y_i^t/y^t	r_i^t/r^t	$_iV^t/V^t$
Correlation between independent and dependent variable	0.20	-0.28	-0.49
Regression coefficient	0.367	-0.580	-0.399
Standard error of regression coefficient	0.390	1.970	0.331
Computed t-value	0.941	-0.294	-1.203

Coefficient of multiple correlation $= 0.54$

Secondly, and this is very important, because the η-estimate and the ϑ-estimate are negative.

7   To improve the results, we exclude from the analysis the 1880-data for the West South Central and the Mountain regions and the 1900-data for the West North Central and the Mountain regions. In these four cases the difference between the observed and the estimated value of the dependent variable is greater than 0.5000. This is, in fact, the only reason for excluding them. We want a better statistical fit. In an ordinary, respectable statistical analysis such a procedure would not have been permissible. To exclude certain regions at certain points of time from the analysis could only be justified by presenting evidence for those special circumstances that made these regions atypical at the given points of time. Keeping in mind the low level of ambition of what we are doing in this chapter, we shall not justify the exclusion further.

We now do a second multiple regression analysis on the remaining 14 sets of observations. The result is shown in table 6.6. The computed t-values are better and the coefficient of multiple

TABLE 6.6

Results of the second multiple regression analysis.

	20ζ	20η	20ϑ
Independent variable	y_i^t/y^t	r_i^t/r^t	$_iV^t/V^t$
Correlation between independent and dependent variable	0.31	-0.22	-0.54
Regression coefficient	0.613	-1.745	-0.183
Standard error of regression coefficient	0.280	1.344	0.177
Computed t-value	2.191	-1.298	-1.032

Coefficient of multiple correlation = 0.73

correlation has increased to 0.73. The signs of η and ϑ are, however, still negative. This is serious.

8 In chapter 3 paragraph 13 we assumed that both ζ, η and ϑ were positive.

Behind the assumption of a positive ζ is a theory of capital formation. It was supposed that regions with relatively high per capita incomes would add relatively more to their capital stocks. The positive ζ thus expresses one of the disequilibrating forces in the economy. This part of our theory is confirmed by the regression analysis.

9 The theory behind the assumption of a positive η is that capital will move from regions where the rate of return is relatively low to regions where it is relatively high. Thus, the positive η-value should express one of the equilibrating forces of the economy. But, the regression analysis tells us that η is negative.

Let us suppose that the estimate of η is a correct one. How should we then interpret the negative sign of the parameter?

One possibility is to give up the Heckscher–Ohlin theory

behind the assumption of a positive η-value. Instead we could accept the Myrdal theory telling us that capital moves from the poor to the rich regions for the reasons mentioned in chapter 2, paragraph 44.

Another possibility is to stick to the Heckscher–Ohlin theory and to emphasize the friction of distance. This friction might limit the interregional capital movements so much that the capital stock, despite capital exports, grows relatively faster in the rich regions. Correspondingly, the capital stock might grow relatively slowly in the poorer regions, despite capital imports. This might lead to a downward pressure on the rate of return on capital in the rich regions and an upward pressure in the poor regions. Thus, the negative η-value should express how much stronger a disequilibrating force, i.e. the friction of distance, is than an equilibrating one, i.e. the conventional interregional capital movements. Let us accept this interpretation.

10 Let us now suppose that η can be disaggregated into two components, η_m and η_f.

$$\eta = \eta_m + \eta_f, \tag{6.7}$$

where

$$\eta < 0, \tag{6.8}$$

$$\eta_m > 0, \tag{6.9}$$

$$\eta_f < 0. \tag{6.10}$$

η_m is that part of η which is related to the capital movements. It is positive because it expresses the fact that capital to some extent moves to regions with higher rates of return.

η_f is that part of η which is related to the friction of distance. It is negative because it expresses that the friction of distance to some extent keeps capital at home. This makes the growth of capital relatively high and the rate of return relatively low in the richer regions.

11   Now, we can turn to the theory behind the assumption of a positive ϑ-value. From chapter 3 paragraph 13, we remember that ϑ was made a corollary to ϑ. The positive value of ϑ should tell us that capital moved into a region if the regional rate of return was higher than the national average and out of the region if it was lower. The positive value of ϑ should tell us that the speed of the response varied directly with the relative level of interaction between the region and the rest of the nation.

Wanting to uphold the Heckscher–Ohlin theory of inter-regional capital movements we shall regard ϑ as a corollary to η_m which is positive. We then expect a positive value of ϑ. But the regression analysis gives us a negative one. How could this be explained?

12   One possible explanation is that the estimate is a wrong one. Let us suppose that this is not the case. Another possibility is that there are many other ways from the relative level of inter-action to the growth of the regional capital stock. Let us also disregard this possibility.

Trying to find an explanation, we could start with a look at table 6.7. This tells us that we have to find the explanation out-side conventional economic theory. So we turn to Gunnar Myrdal. He writes about the inclination of capitalists to invest in high income regions with stable organized capital markets and relatively low rates of return. They feel more comfortable when their capital is invested in rich regions and they are willing to pay for this comfort, i.e. to accept lower rates of return than they could have obtained investing in poor regions. Let us try to accept this Myrdal hypothesis. Let us further suppose that the more a capitalist knows about the regional differences, i.e. the higher the level of interaction between his region and the rest of the nation is, the more marked is his preference for investing in the rich regions.

TABLE 6.7
Effects of ϑ on regional capital exports and imports.

	$\vartheta > 0$		$\vartheta < 0$	
	$_iV^t/V^t > 1$	$_iV^t/V^t < 1$	$_iV^t/V^t > 1$	$_iV^t/V^t < 1$
	(1)	(2)	(3)	(4)
Export of capital from regions where $r_i^t/r^t < 1$	Positive	Negative	Negative	Positive
Import of capital into regions where $r_i^t/r^t > 1$	Positive	Negative	Negative	Positive

The two above-mentioned hypotheses explain column (3) of table 6.7. If the level of interaction is relatively high the biases for investing in the rich regions will be strong. This will reduce the net capital exports from the rich regions. For two reasons: firstly, because the capitalists of the rich regions to a great extent might prefer to let their capital stay at home. Secondly, because capitalists of the poor regions to some extent might prefer to invest their capital in the rich regions. For the same reasons the net capital imports into the poor regions will be reduced.

To explain column (4) of table 6.7 is more than difficult. So we do not.

13 In fact, the explanation of the negative ϑ-value was not very convincing. This leaves us with two alternatives. The one is to go on with the analysis as if the explanation had been satisfactory. The other is to delete the variable $(_iV^t/V^t)$ from the analysis of the growth of the regional capital stocks. This can be done by giving ϑ the value zero.

If the relative level of interaction is excluded from the analysis a third regression analysis is needed. Table 6.8 shows the results.

Like the second analysis, it was done without the 1880-data for the West South Central and the Mountain regions and the 1900-data for the West North Central and the Mountain regions.

TABLE 6.8
Results of the third multiple regression analysis.

	ζ	η
Independent variable	y_i^t/y^t	r_i^t/r^t
Correlation between independent and dependent variable	0.31	-0.22
Regression coefficient	0.755	-2.741
Standard error of regression coefficient	0.245	0.938
Computed t-value	3.084	-2.921

Coefficient of multiple correlation $= 0.70$

We note that the exclusion of the level of interaction has only reduced the coefficient of multiple correlation from 0.73 to 0.70. The t-values are, however, far better than those given in table 6.6.

14 In the following we shall work with both alternatives. So we end up with two sets of preliminary estimates:

Alternative 1:

$$\zeta = 0.0307; \quad \eta = -0.0873 \text{ and } \vartheta = -0.0091.$$

Alternative 2:

$$\zeta = 0.0377 \quad \text{and} \quad \eta = -0.1370.$$

The parameter Θ

15 We now turn to eq. (3.12) determining the growth of regional labour forces. Our first task is to try to estimate the value of the parameter Θ. This is done on the basis of the national L-values from table 5.4, column (3) and eq. (6.11).

$$e^{70\Theta} = \frac{L^{1949-51}}{L^{1880}},$$
(6.11)

which gives us the preliminary estimate:

$$\Theta = 0.0177.$$

The parameters H, λ and μ

16 Our next task is to try to estimate the values of the parameters H, λ and μ. We hope that this can be done in two multiple regression analyses where eqs. (6.12) and (6.13) are used instead of eq. (3.12)

$$L_i^{t+20} = L_i^t \, e^{20\Theta} \left(\frac{y_i^t}{y^t}\right)^{20H} \left(\frac{w_i^t}{w^t}\right)^{20\lambda} \left(\frac{_iV^t}{V^t}\right)^{20\mu},$$
(6.12)

is used for $t = 1880$ and $t = 1900$.

$$L_i^{t+30} = L_i^t \, e^{30\Theta} \left(\frac{y_i^t}{y^t}\right)^{30H} \left(\frac{w_i^t}{w^t}\right)^{30\lambda} \left(\frac{_iV^t}{V^t}\right)^{30\mu},$$
(6.13)

is used for $t = 1919-21$.

Eqs. (6.12) and (6.13) are given the following forms:

$$\left(\frac{y_i^t}{y^t}\right)^{20H} \left(\frac{w_i^t}{w^t}\right)^{20\lambda} \left(\frac{_iV^t}{V^t}\right)^{20\mu} = \frac{L_i^{t+20}}{L_i^t e^{20\Theta}},$$
(6.14)

and

$$\left(\frac{y^t}{y_i^t}\right)^{30H} \left(\frac{w_i^t}{w^t}\right)^{30\lambda} \left(\frac{{}_iV^t}{V^t}\right)^{30\mu} = \frac{L_i^{t+30}}{L_i^t e^{300}}. \tag{6.15}$$

The data to be used in the multiple regression analyses are given in table 6.9.

The results shown in table 6.10 are not too bad. The signs of H and λ are positive ones and the coefficient of multiple

TABLE 6.9

Data to be used in the estimation of H, λ and μ.

	$\dfrac{y^t}{y_i^t}$	$\dfrac{w_i^t}{w^t}$	$\dfrac{{}_iV^t}{V^t}$	$\dfrac{L_i^{t+20}}{L_i^t\, e^{200}}$
$t = 1880$	(1)	(2)	(3)	(4)
1. New England	0.807	1.205	1.577	1.0609
2. Middle Atlantic	0.745	1.317	2.120	1.1481
3. East North Central	0.904	1.103	1.380	1.1431
4. West North Central	1.022	0.990	0.777	1.2917
5. South Atlantic	2.214	0.459	0.865	1.0509
6. East South Central	1.875	0.551	1.003	1.0805
7. West South Central	1.632	0.642	0.618	1.4207
8. Mountain	0.716	1.495	0.356	1.6440
9. Pacific	0.603	1.720	0.302	1.5445
$t = 1900$				
1. New England	0.845	1.180	1.499	0.9541
2. Middle Atlantic	0.779	1.254	2.042	1.0348
3. East North Central	0.896	1.119	1.398	1.0139
4. West North Central	0.932	1.082	0.820	0.8710
5. South Atlantic	2.158	0.478	0.854	0.9257
6. East South Central	2.006	0.524	1.001	0.8033
7. West South Central	1.513	0.677	0.670	1.1240
8. Mountain	0.699	1.440	0.388	1.3262
9. Pacific	0.697	1.424	0.328	1.6273

TABLE 6.9 (*continued*)

				$\dfrac{L_i^{t+30}}{L_i^t \, e^{300}}$
t = 1919–21				
1. New England	0.924	1.077	1.445	0.7097
2. Middle Atlantic	0.827	1.206	2.009	0.8134
3. East North Central	0.913	1.096	1.392	0.8608
4. West North Central	1.025	0.946	0.815	0.7116
5. South Atlantic	1.515	0.666	0.883	0.9067
6. East South Central	1.744	0.598	1.013	0.7292
7. West South Central	1.282	0.803	0.683	0.8522
8. Mountain	0.901	1.106	0.406	0.8905
9. Pacific	0.814	1.218	0.356	1.4614

Sources: y^t/y_i^t: computed as $(Y^t/L^t)/(Y_i^t/L_i^t)$ using data from table 5.1, column (6) and table 5.4, column (3). w_i^t/w^t: table 5.4, column (4). $_iV^t/V^t$: table 5.11. L_i^t: table 5.4, column (3). Θ: the estimate in paragraph 15 above.

correlation is not unsatisfactory. But we should not mind getting some better results and, especially, we should like to see a positive μ-value.

17 To improve the results we exclude from the analysis all cases where the difference between the observed and the estimated value of the dependent variable for *t* = 1880 and *t* = 1900 exceeds 0.1500, i.e. the 1880-data for the Middle Atlantic and the West South Central regions and the 1900-data for the West North Central, the East South Central and the Pacific regions. We then do a second multiple regression analysis. The results are shown in table 6.11. The coefficient of multiple correlation has increased from 0.80 to 0.91, but the computed *t*-values for H and λ are rather poor.

For *t* = 1919–21 we have only 9 sets of observations. Therefore, we do not try to improve the estimates by excluding some of the observations from the analysis.

TABLE 6.10

Results of the first multiple regression analyses.

$t = 1880$ and 1900	20 H	20 λ	20 μ
Independent variable	y^t/y_i^t	w_i^t/w^t	$_iV^t/V^t$
Correlation between independent and dependent variable	-0.45	0.56	-0.57
Regression coefficient	0.044	0.416	-0.247
Standard error of regression coefficient	0.266	0.379	0.083
Computed t-value	0.167	1.098	-2.983
Coefficient of multiple correlation $= 0.80$			
$t = 1919\text{--}21$	30 H	30 λ	30 μ
Independent variable	y^t/y_i^t	w_i^t/w^t	$_iV^t/V^t$
Correlation between independent and dependent variable	-0.32	0.39	-0.50
Regression coefficient	1.468	2.601	-0.291
Standard error of regression coefficient	0.862	1.258	0.112
Computed t-value	1.703	2.068	-2.592
Coefficient of multiple correlation $= 0.83$			

Our estimates are then made as the weighted averages of the results given for $t = 1880$ and 1900 in table 6.11 (weight: two-thirds) and the results given for $t = 1919$–21 in table 6.10 (weight: one-third).

Thus, our preliminary estimates are: H $= 0.0155$, $\lambda = 0.0384$ and $\mu = -0.0123$. So we did not get rid of the negative value of μ. This is unpleasant.

18 The theory behind the assumption of a positive μ-value is exactly the same as the one behind the assumption of a positive

TABLE 6.11

Results of the second multiple regression analysis for $t = 1880$ and 1900.

$t = 1880$ and 1900	20 H	20 λ	20 μ
Independent variable	y^t/y_i^t	w_i^t/w^t	$_iV^t/V^t$
Correlation between independent			
and dependent variable	-0.49	0.65	-0.71
Regression coefficient	-0.025	0.286	-0.272
Standard error of regression			
coefficient	0.193	0.276	0.070
Computed t-value	-0.130	1.038	-3.854

Coefficient of multiple correlation = 0.91

ϑ-value. Therefore, we shall look for an explanation in table 6.12 which is made in the same way as table 6.7 above.

Again, our impression is that the explanation of the negative μ-value should be found outside conventional economic theory. But it is also our impression that it is more than difficult to find a reasonable one.

TABLE 6.12

Effects of μ on regional out-migration and in-migration of labour.

	$\mu > 0$		$\mu < 0$	
	$\dfrac{_iV^t}{V^t} > 1$	$\dfrac{_iV^t}{V^t} < 1$	$\dfrac{_iV^t}{V^t} > 1$	$\dfrac{_iV^t}{V^t} < 1$
Out-migration of labour from regions where $w_i^t/w^t < 1$	Positive	Negative	Negative	Positive
In-migration of labour into regions where $w_i^t/w^t > 1$	Positive	Negative	Negative	Positive

19   This leaves us with two alternatives: either we could go on accepting that μ is negative without being able to explain why, or, we could exclude the variable $(_iV^t/V^t)$ from the analysis of the growth of the regional labour forces. This can be done by giving μ the value zero.

If the relative level of interaction is excluded from the analysis a third multiple regression analysis is necessary. Table 6.13 gives the results of one using the same data as the second multiple regression analysis for $t = 1880$ and $t = 1900$ and the same data as the first one for $t = 1919$–21.

Our estimates are then made as the weighted averages of the

TABLE 6.13
Results of the third multiple regression analysis.

$t = 1880$ and 1900	20 H	20 λ
Independent variable	y^t/y_i^t	w_i^t/w^t
Correlation between independent		
and dependent variable	-0.49	0.65
Regression coefficient	0.425	0.931
Standard error of regression		
coefficient	0.238	0.339
Computed t-value	1.790	2.744
Coefficient of multiple correlation $= 0.75$		
$t = 1919$–21	30 H	30 λ
Independent variable	y^t/y_i^t	w_i^t/w^t
Correlation between independent		
and dependent variable	-0.32	0.39
Regression coefficient	1.075	1.918
Standard error of regression		
coefficient	1.186	1.719
Computed t-value	0.906	1.116
Coefficient of multiple correlation $= 0.51$		

results given for $t = 1880$ and 1900 (weight: two-thirds) and the results given for $t = 1919$–21 (weight: one-third).

Thus, our alternative preliminary estimates are: $H = 0.0261$ and $\lambda = 0.0523$.

20　In the following, we shall work with both alternatives. So we end up with two sets of preliminary estimates:

Alternative 1:

$$H = 0.0155; \quad \lambda = 0.0384 \quad \text{and} \quad \mu = -0.0123.$$

Alternative 2:

$$H = 0.0261 \quad \text{and} \quad \lambda = 0.0523.$$

The parameter Λ

21　We now turn to eq. (3.14) determining regional growth in productivity. Our first task is to try to estimate the value of the parameter Λ. This estimate is made on the basis of the national γ-values given in table 6.3 and eq. (6.16).

$$e^{40\Lambda} = \frac{\gamma^{1919-21}}{\gamma^{1880}}, \tag{6.16}$$

which gives us the preliminary estimate:

$$\Lambda = 0.0113.$$

The parameters v, π and τ

22　Our next task is to try to estimate the values of the parameters v, π and τ. We should like to do this in a multiple regression analysis where eq. (6.17) is used instead of eq. (3.14).

$$\gamma_i^{t+20} = \gamma_i^t e^{20\Lambda} \left(\frac{E_i^t}{E^t}\right)^{20v} \left(\frac{U_i^t}{U^t}\right)^{20\pi} \left(\frac{{}_iV^t}{V^t}\right)^{20\tau}. \tag{6.17}$$

Eq. (6.17) is given the form:

$$\left(\frac{E_i^t}{E^t}\right)^{20\nu} \left(\frac{U_i^t}{U^t}\right)^{20\pi} \left(\frac{{}_iV^t}{V^t}\right)^{20\tau} = \frac{\gamma_i^{t+20}}{\gamma_i^t e^{20\Lambda}}. \qquad (6.18)$$

The data to be used in the multiple regression analysis are given in table 6.14.

TABLE 6.14
Data to be used in the estimation of ν, π and τ.

	$\dfrac{E_i^t}{E^t}$	$\dfrac{U_i^t}{U^t}$	$\dfrac{{}_iV^t}{V^t}$	$\dfrac{\gamma_i^{t+20}}{\gamma_i^t e^{20\Lambda}}$
$t = 1880$	(1)	(2)	(3)	(4)
1. New England	1.030	1.871	1.577	0.9121
2. Middle Atlantic	1.030	1.757	2.120	0.8914
3. East North Central	0.985	0.982	1.380	0.9557
4. West North Central	1.000	0.650	0.777	0.9884
5. South Atlantic	0.940	0.307	0.865	0.9780
6. East South Central	0.955	0.300	1.003	0.9105
7. West South Central	0.910	0.446	0.618	0.9714
8. Mountain	1.015	0.771	0.356	0.8804
9. Pacific	1.030	1.293	0.302	0.7904
$t = 1900$				
1. New England	1.030	1.737	1.499	0.9976
2. Middle Atlantic	1.030	1.618	2.042	1.0440
3. East North Central	0.985	1.144	1.398	1.0613
4. West North Central	1.000	0.722	0.820	0.9666
5. South Atlantic	0.940	0.367	0.854	1.4110
6. East South Central	0.955	0.380	1.001	1.2070
7. West South Central	0.910	0.410	0.670	1.2597
8. Mountain	1.015	0.820	0.388	0.8699
9. Pacific	1.030	1.175	0.328	0.9407

Sources: E_i^t/E^t: since we have no data for educational attainment in 1880 and 1900, we use in both cases the 1910-data from table 5.7. U_i^t/U^t: table 5.9. ${}_iV^t/V^t$: table 5.11. γ_i^t: table 6.3. Λ: the estimate in paragraph 21 above.

The results shown in table 6.15 are by no means encouraging. The coefficient of multiple correlation is 0.64 and the signs of both ν and π are negative.

TABLE 6.15
Results of the first multiple regression analysis.

	$20\,\nu$	$20\,\pi$	$20\,\tau$
Independent variable	E_i^t/E^t	U_i^t/U^t	$_iV^t/V^t$
Correlation between independent and dependent variable	-0.59	-0.41	0.07
Regression coefficient	-2.050	-0.030	0.077
Standard error of regression coefficient	1.448	0.137	0.080
Computed t-value	-1.416	-0.219	0.964

Coefficient of multiple correlation $= 0.64$

23   To improve the results we exclude from the analysis all the cases where the differences between the observed and the estimated value of the dependent variable exceeds 0.1000. The excluded data are the 1880-data for the South Atlantic, the East South Central and the West South Central regions, and the 1900-data for the same regions. The results of the second regression analysis are given in table 6.16. The coefficient of multiple correlation has increased from 0.64 to 0.68 which is modest and the computed t-values are far from being satisfactory. The signs of ν and π remain negative.

24   Table 6.16 indicates that it might not be a bad idea to assume a zero value for π, i.e. to exclude the relative level of urbanization from the analysis. This is done and a third multiple regression analysis is made on the basis of data from the same regions and at the same times as the second multiple regression analysis. The results are shown in table 6.17. The exclusion of

Table 6.16
Results of the second multiple regression analysis.

	$20\,\nu$	$20\,\pi$	$20\,\tau$
Independent variable	E_i^t/E^t	U_i^t/U^t	$_iV^t/V^t$
Correlation between independent and dependent variable	-0.40	0.05	0.50
Regression coefficient	-1.242	-0.045	0.082
Standard error of regression coefficient	2.029	0.116	0.058
Computed t-value	-0.612	-0.391	1.417

Coefficient of multiple correlation $= 0.68$

the relative level of urbanization has reduced the coefficient of multiple correlation from 0.68 to 0.67, but the computed t-values are far better than those given in table 6.16. However, our main problem has not been solved. The value of ν is still negative. How can this be explained?

Table 6.17
Results of the third multiple regression analysis.

	$20\,\nu$	$20\,\tau$
Independent variable	E_i^t/E^t	$_iV^t/V^t$
Correlation between independent and dependent variable	-0.40	0.50
Regression coefficient	-1.906	0.062
Standard error of regression coefficient	1.061	0.029
Computed t-value	-1.796	2.183

Coefficient of multiple correlation $= 0.67$

25 The theory behind the assumption of a positive value of v is that the higher a region's relative level of education is, the more rapidly are new production methods accepted. This is however, not incompatible with a negative value of v. The slow change of production methods in regions with a low level of education might well increase productivity relatively more than the fast change in regions with a high level of education. There might be decreasing returns to investment in education.

26 Let us then, as one of two possibilities, accept the negative value of v and the zero value of π. This gives us the following preliminary estimates:

$$v = -0.0953, \quad \pi = 0.0000 \quad \text{and} \quad \tau = 0.0031.$$

A new equation with a parameter κ

27 The other possibility is to give up eq. (3.14) and try to find better determinants of the regional growth in productivity than education, urbanization and interaction.

We shall look for a simple explanation. Doing this, it seems rather meaningless to work with as complicated a production function as the CES function. And since the σ-values given in table 6.1 are very close to 1, we shall work with the Cobb–Douglas function:

$$Y_i^t = \gamma_i^t (K_i^t)^{\delta_i} (L_i^t)^{1-\delta_i}. \tag{6.19}$$

Table 6.18 gives the values of the efficiency parameters in this function. The estimates are made on the Y-values from table 5.1 column (6), the K-values from table 5.3, column (3), the L-values from table 5.4, column (3) and the δ-estimates given in table 6.2.

28 Having other γ-values we shall need a new estimate of the parameter Λ indicating the annual rate of growth in US product-

TABLE 6.18
Estimates of the γ-values in the Cobb–Douglas model.

	1880	1900	1919–21
0. United States	$\gamma = 115$	$\gamma = 131$	$\gamma = 175$
1. New England	$\gamma_1 = 133$	$\gamma_1 = 151$	$\gamma_1 = 188$
2. Middle Atlantic	$\gamma_2 = 100$	$\gamma_2 = 108$	$\gamma_2 = 142$
3. East North Central	$\gamma_3 = 111$	$\gamma_3 = 130$	$\gamma_3 = 173$
4. West North Central	$\gamma_4 = 96$	$\gamma_4 = 114$	$\gamma_4 = 136$
5. South Atlantic	$\gamma_5 = 94$	$\gamma_5 = 114$	$\gamma_5 = 200$
6. East South Central	$\gamma_6 = 127$	$\gamma_6 = 143$	$\gamma_6 = 214$
7. West South Central	$\gamma_7 = 144$	$\gamma_7 = 175$	$\gamma_7 = 275$
8. Mountain	$\gamma_8 = 212$	$\gamma_8 = 227$	$\gamma_8 = 248$
9. Pacific	$\gamma_9 = 135$	$\gamma_9 = 128$	$\gamma_9 = 152$

ivity. This estimate on the national γ-values given in table 6.18 and eq. (6.20)

$$e^{40\Lambda} = \frac{\gamma^{1919-21}}{\gamma^{1880}} \tag{6.20}$$

gives us the preliminary estimate

$$\Lambda = 0.0106.$$

29 We are now ready for the new and more simple explanation of the regional growth in productivity. We shall assume a correlation between the growth in productivity and the relative level of per capita income. This is done in equation

$$\gamma_i^{t+20} = \gamma_i^t e^{20\Lambda} \left(\frac{y_i^t}{y^t}\right)^{20\kappa}$$

which can be given the form:

$$\left(\frac{y_i^t}{y^t}\right)^{20\kappa} = \frac{\gamma_i^{t+20}}{\gamma_i^t e^{20\Lambda}}. \tag{6.21}$$

The value of κ can then be estimated in a regression analysis. The data to be used are given in table 6.19.

TABLE 6.19
Data to be used in the estimation of κ.

	$\dfrac{y_i^t}{y^t}$	$\dfrac{\gamma_i^{t+20}}{\gamma_i^t e^{20\Lambda}}$
$t = 1880$	(1)	(2)
1. New England	1.239	0.9183
2. Middle Atlantic	1.343	0.8738
3. East North Central	1.106	0.9475
4. West North Central	0.978	0.9604
5. South Atlantic	0.452	0.9806
6. East South Central	0.533	0.9110
7. West South Central	0.613	0.9831
8. Mountain	1.397	0.8665
9. Pacific	1.657	0.7671
$t = 1900$		
1. New England	1.184	1.0073
2. Middle Atlantic	1.284	1.0639
3. East North Central	1.116	1.0769
4. West North Central	1.073	0.9653
5. South Atlantic	0.463	1.4192
6. East South Central	0.499	1.2112
7. West South Central	0.661	1.2711
8. Mountain	1.431	0.8843
9. Pacific	1.436	0.9612

Sources: y_i^t/y^t: computed as $(Y_i^t/L_i^t)/(Y^t/L^t)$ using the data from table 5.1, column (6) and table 5.4, column (3). γ_i^t: table 6.18. Λ: the estimate in paragraph 28 above.

The results of the analysis are given in table 6.20. They are by no means unsatisfactory but there should be room for improvements.

30 To improve the results, we exclude from the analysis all cases where the difference between the observed and the esti-

TABLE 6.20
Results of the first regression analysis.

	20κ
Independent variable	y_i^t/y^t
Coefficient of correlation	-0.64
Regression coefficient	-0.262
Standard error of regression coefficient	0.077
Computed t-value	-3.385

mated value of the dependent variable exceeds 0.1000. The excluded data are the 1880-data for the South Atlantic, the East South Central and the West South Central regions and the 1900-data for the Middle Atlantic, the South Atlantic and the West South Atlantic and the West South Central regions. We then do a second regression analysis. The results are given in table 6.21. We thus end up with the preliminary estimate

$$\kappa = -0.0170.$$

31 Under the assumptions given above, we need no equation for education and no equation for urbanization. All we need are

TABLE 6.21
Results of the second regression analysis.

	$20\,\kappa$
Independent variable	y_i^t/y^t
Coefficient of correlation	-0.89
Regression coefficient	-0.340
Standard error of regression coefficient	0.056
Computed t-value	-6.114

eqs. (6.22) to (6.25).

$$Y_i^t = \gamma_i^t (K_i^t)^{\delta_i} (L_i^t)^{1-\delta_i}, \tag{6.22}$$

$$K_i^{t+1} = K_i^t e^{\Gamma} \left(\frac{y_i^t}{y^t}\right)^{\zeta} \left(\frac{r_i^t}{r^t}\right)^{\eta}, \tag{6.23}$$

$$L_i^{t+1} = L_i^t e^{\Theta} \left(\frac{y_i^t}{y_i^t}\right)^{H} \left(\frac{w_i^t}{w^t}\right)^{\lambda}, \tag{6.24}$$

and

$$\gamma_i^{t+1} = \gamma_i^t e^{\Lambda} \left(\frac{y_i^t}{y^t}\right)^{\kappa}. \tag{6.25}$$

This simplified Cobb–Douglas model is our alternative to the full CES model. In the following we shall work with both models.

The parameter Ξ

32   Returning to the full CES model, we shall try to estimate the parameter Ξ of eq. (3.17). This is done using the national E-values from table 5.7 and eq. (6.26).

$$e^{40\Xi} = \frac{E^{1950}}{E^{1910}}. \tag{6.26}$$

This gives us the preliminary estimate

$$\Xi = 0.0089.$$

The parameters v, φ and χ

33   Going on with eq. (3.17), we shall now try to estimate the parameters v, φ and χ. This is done using eq. (6.27) as an approximation to eq. (3.17).

$$E_i^{t+30} = E_i^t e^{30\Xi} \left(\frac{y_i^t}{y^t}\right)^{30v} \left(\frac{U_i^t}{U^t}\right)^{30\varphi} \left(\frac{{}_iV^t}{V^t}\right)^{30\chi}, \tag{6.27}$$

which can be given the form:

$$\left(\frac{y_i^t}{y^t}\right)^{30v}\left(\frac{U_i^t}{U^t}\right)^{30\varphi}\left(\frac{{}_iV^t}{V^t}\right)^{30\chi} = \frac{E_i^{t+30}}{E_i^t e^{30\Xi}}. \tag{6.28}$$

It should then be possible to estimate the values of v, φ and χ in a multiple regression analysis. The data to be used are given in table 6.22.

TABLE 6.22
Data to be used in the estimation of v, φ and χ.

$t = 1919–21$	$\dfrac{y_i^t}{y^t}$	$\dfrac{U_i^t}{U^t}$	$\dfrac{{}_iV^t}{V^t}$	$\dfrac{E_i^{t+30}}{E_i^t e^{30\Xi}}$
	(1)	(2)	(3)	(4)
1. New England	1.083	1.488	1.445	1.1031
2. Middle Atlantic	1.209	1.457	2.009	1.0014
3. East North Central	1.095	1.192	1.392	1.0954
4. West North Central	0.976	0.739	0.815	1.0304
5. South Atlantic	0.660	0.480	0.883	0.9614
6. East South Central	0.573	0.439	1.013	0.9219
7. West South Central	0.780	0.569	0.683	1.0194
8. Mountain	1.110	0.716	0.406	1.1634
9. Pacific	1.229	1.220	0.356	1.2105

Sources: y_i^t/y^t: computed as $(Y_i^t/L_i^t)/(Y^t/L^t)$ using the data from table 5.1, column (6) and table 5.4, column (3). U_i^t/U^t: table 5.9. ${}_iV^t/V^t$: table 5.11. E_i^t: table 5.7. Ξ: the estimate in paragraph 32 above.

The results of the analysis are given in table 6.23. They are not unsatisfactory although we had hoped to get a positive value of the χ-estimate. So, we shall not try to improve them by excluding some of the only nine sets of observations. The preliminary estimates are the following:

$$v = 0.0054, \quad \varphi = 0.0046 \quad \text{and} \quad \chi = -0.0038.$$

TABLE 6.23
Results of the first regression analysis.

	$30\,v$	$30\,\varphi$	$30\,\chi$
Independent variable	y_i^t/y^t	U_i^t/U^t	$_iV^t/V^t$
Correlation between independent and dependent variable	0.78	0.50	-0.39
Regression coefficient	0.162	0.139	-0.143
Standard error of regression coefficient	0.101	0.070	0.031
Computed t-value	1.597	1.982	-4.644

Coefficient of multiple correlation $= 0.97$

34 Having estimated the values of v, φ and χ we should be able to estimate the values of E^{1880} and E_i^{1880} which we shall need as status variables. This is done by giving eqs. (6.26) and (6.27) the following forms:

$$E^{1880} = \frac{E^{1910}}{e^{30\Xi}}, \tag{6.29}$$

and

$$E_i^{1880} = \frac{E_i^{1910}}{e^{30\Xi}\left(\frac{y_i^{1880}}{y^{1880}}\right)^{30v}\left(\frac{U_i^{1880}}{U^{1880}}\right)^{30\varphi}\left(\frac{_iV^{1880}}{V^{1880}}\right)^{30\chi}}. \tag{6.30}$$

The results are shown in table 6.24.

The parameter Ω

35 Finally, we shall turn to eq. (3.18). Our first task is to try to estimate the parameter Ω. This is done on the basis of the national U-values from table 5.9 and eq. (6.31).

$$e^{80\Omega} = \frac{U^{1950}}{U^{1870}}. \tag{6.31}$$

TABLE 6.24
Estimated values of E and E_i $(i = 1, 2, \ldots, 9)$
in 1880.

	1880
0. United States	$E = 5.1$ years
1. New England	$E_1 = 5.2$ years
2. Middle Atlantic	$E_2 = 5.4$ years
3. East North Central	$E_3 = 5.1$ years
4. West North Central	$E_4 = 5.2$ years
5. South Atlantic	$E_5 = 5.6$ years
6. East South Central	$E_6 = 6.0$ years
7. West South Central	$E_7 = 5.0$ years
8. Mountain	$E_8 = 4.7$ years
9. Pacific	$E_9 = 4.3$ years

This gives the preliminary estimate

$$\Omega = 0.0104.$$

The parameters ψ and ω

36 Our last task is to try to estimate the parameters ψ and ω. It is hoped that this can be done in two multiple regression analyses where eqs. (6.32) and (6.33) are used as approximations to eq. (3.18).

$$U_i^{t+20} = U_i^t e^{20\Omega} \left(\frac{y_i^t}{y^t}\right)^{20\psi} \left(\frac{_iV^t}{V^t}\right)^{20\omega}, \tag{6.32}$$

is used for $t = 1880$ and 1900 and

$$U_i^{t+30} = U_i^t e^{30\Omega} \left(\frac{y_i^t}{y^t}\right)^{30\psi} \left(\frac{_iV^t}{V^t}\right)^{30\omega}, \tag{6.33}$$

is used for $t = 1919$–21.

Eqs. (6.32) and (6.33) are given the forms:

$$\left(\frac{y_i^t}{y^t}\right)^{20\psi}\left(\frac{{}_iV^t}{V^t}\right)^{20\omega} = \frac{U_i^{t+20}}{U_i^t e^{20\Omega}},\tag{6.34}$$

and

$$\left(\frac{y_i^t}{y^t}\right)^{30\psi}\left(\frac{{}_iV^t}{V^t}\right)^{30\omega} = \frac{U_i^{t+30}}{U_i^t e^{30\Omega}}.\tag{6.35}$$

The data to be used in the multiple regression analyses are given in table 6.25 and the results are shown in table 6.26. We

TABLE 6.25
Data to be used in the estimation of ψ and ω.

	$\dfrac{y_i^t}{y^t}$	$\dfrac{{}_iV^t}{V^t}$	$\dfrac{U_i^{t+20}}{U_i^t e^{20\Omega}}$
$t = 1880$	(1)	(2)	(3)
1. New England	1.239	1.577	1.0626
2. Middle Atlantic	1.343	2.120	1.0542
3. East North Central	1.106	1.380	1.3341
4. West North Central	0.978	0.777	1.2711
5. South Atlantic	0.452	0.865	1.3685
6. East South Central	0.533	1.003	1.4494
7. West South Central	0.613	0.618	1.0519
8. Mountain	1.397	0.356	1.2175
9. Pacific	1.657	0.302	1.0404
$t = 1900$			
1. New England	1.184	1.499	0.8981
2. Middle Atlantic	1.284	2.042	0.9438
3. East North Central	1.116	1.398	1.0918
4. West North Central	1.073	0.820	1.0737
5. South Atlantic	0.463	0.854	1.3415
6. East South Central	0.499	1.001	1.2121
7. West South Central	0.661	0.670	1.4530
8. Mountain	1.431	0.388	0.9144
9. Pacific	1.436	0.328	1.0881

TABLE 6.25 *(continued)*

			$\dfrac{U_i^{t+30}}{U_i^t e^{30\Omega}}$
$t = 1919\text{--}21$			
1. New England	1.083	1.445	0.7156
2. Middle Atlantic	1.209	2.009	0.7212
3. East North Central	1.095	1.392	0.7899
4. West North Central	0.976	0.815	0.9675
5. South Atlantic	0.660	0.883	1.1398
6. East South Central	0.573	1.013	1.1585
7. West South Central	0.780	0.683	1.3360
8. Mountain	1.110	0.406	0.9773
9. Pacific	1.229	0.356	0.7392

Sources: y_i^t/y^t: computed as $(Y_i^t/L_i^t)/(Y^t/L^t)$ using the data from table 5.1, column (6) and table 5.4, column (3). $_iV^t/V^t$: table 5.11. U_i^t: table 5.9. Ω: the estimate in paragraph 35 above.

had expected both ψ and ω to be positive, but we shall not try to improve the estimates for $t = 1919\text{--}21$ by excluding some of the only nine sets of observations. We shall, however, try to improve the estimates for $t = 1880$ and 1900 by excluding all cases

TABLE 6.26
Results of the first multiple regression analyses.

$t = 1880$ and 1900	$20\,\psi$	$20\,\omega$
Independent variable	y_i^t/y^t	$_iV^t/V^t$
Correlation between independent and dependent variable	-0.68	-0.22
Regression coefficient	-0.308	-0.062
Standard error of regression coefficient	0.084	0.059
Computed t-value	-3.666	-1.056
Coefficient of multiple correlation $= 0.71$		

TABLE 6.26 (continued)

$t = 1919\text{--}21$	$30\,\psi$	$30\,\omega$
Independent variable	y_i^t/y^t	$_iV^t/V^t$
Correlation between independent and dependent variable	-0.84	-0.44
Regression coefficient	-0.745	-0.126
Standard error of regression coefficient	0.173	0.078
Computed t-value	-4.307	-1.626

Coefficient of multiple correlation $= 0.90$

where the difference between the observed and the estimated value of the dependent variable exceeds 0.1750. The excluded data are the 1880-data for the East North Central and the West South Central regions and the 1900-data for the Middle Atlantic and the West South Central regions.

37 The results of the second multiple regression analysis are given in table 6.27. The coefficient of multiple correlation has

TABLE 6.27
Results of the second multiple regression analysis for $t = 1880$ and 1900.

$t = 1880$ and 1900	$20\,\psi$	$20\,\omega$
Independent variable	y_i^t/y^t	$_iV^t/V^t$
Correlation between independent and dependent variable	-0.81	-0.20
Regression coefficient	-0.327	-0.071
Standard error of regression coefficient	0.063	0.044
Computed t-value	-5.179	-1.631

Coefficient of multiple correlation $= 0.85$

increased from 0.71 to 0.85 and also the computed t-values have improved.

The estimates of ψ and ω are now computed as weighted averages of the results given in table 6.27 for $t = 1880$ and 1900 (weight: two-thirds) and the results given in table 6.26 for $t = 1919$–21 (weight: one-third). This gives us the preliminary estimates:

$$\psi = -0.0192 \quad \text{and} \quad \omega = -0.038.$$

CHAPTER 7

Alternative 1

1 In this chapter we shall try to run the full CES model using the preliminary "estimates" of the parameters made in chapter 6, i.e., the betas, deltas and gammas, and the exponential parameters presented as alternative 1. For convenience, the latter are repeated in table 7.1.

2 The model constructed in chapter 3 integrates basic elements of different theories of interregional and international trade and related spatial interaction. These elements are more or less supported by evidence presented in serious econometric studies. Our model is constructed in a way making it a fundamental assumption that the exponential parameters are positive. Never-

TABLE 7.1
The estimated values of the exponential parameters.

Code*	Parameter	Value	Code*	Parameter	Value
P 1	Γ	0.0327	P 11	π	0.0000
P 2	ζ	0.0307	P 12	τ	0.0031
P 3	η	−0.0873	P 13	Ξ	0.0089
P 4	ϑ	−0.0091	P 14	υ	0.0054
P 5	Θ	0.0177	P 15	φ	0.0046
P 6	H	0.0155	P 16	χ	−0.0038
P 7	λ	0.0384	P 17	Ω	0.0104
P 8	μ	−0.0123	P 18	ψ	−0.0192
P 9	Λ	0.0113	P 19	ω	−0.0038
P 10	ν	−0.0953			

*The code refers to the computer programme in appendix B.

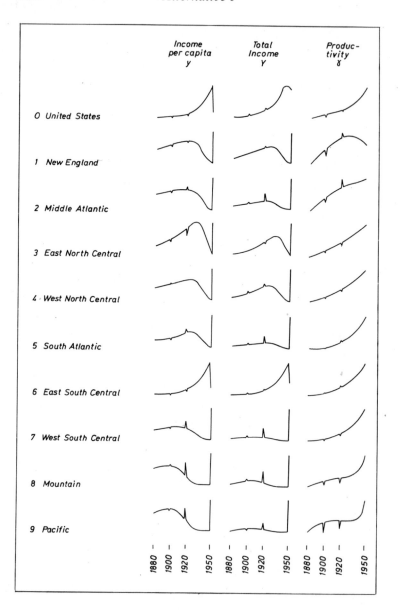

Fig. 7.1.

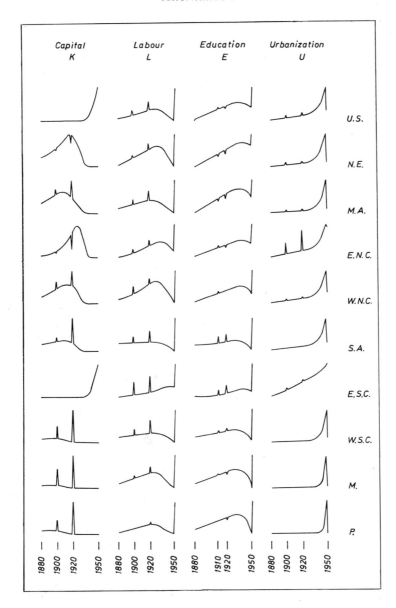

Fig. 7.1 (*continued*).

TABLE 7.2
Maximum and minimum values of the variables in fig. 7.1.

		y	Y	γ	K	L	E	U
		1929 dollars	Millions of 1929 dollars		Millions of 1929 dollars	Millions	Years of school completed	Percent
0. U.S.	Max.	407+1	153+3	477+0	700+6	598−1	940−2	136−0
	Min.	331+0	151+2	151+0	750+2	137−1	510−2	280−1
1. N.E.	Max.	879+0	900+1	250+0	302+2	389−2	101−1	233−0
	Min.	134−1	505−1	175+0	250−6	144−2	520−2	524−1
2. M.A.	Max.	968+0	350+2	225+0	728+2	137−1	930−2	283−0
	Min.	968−3	508−2	154+0	121−8	200−2	540−2	492−1
3. E.N.C.	Max.	965+0	310+2	417+0	218+3	125−1	960−2	681−1
	Min.	118+0	161+1	157+0	394−3	361−2	510−2	275−1
4. W.N.C.	Max.	822+0	120+2	308+0	408+2	556−2	930−2	130−0
	Min.	305−2	127−1	130+0	192−8	158−2	520−2	182−1
5. S.A.	Max.	625+0	112+2	583+0	202+2	680−2	830−2	131−0
	Min.	402−2	763−2	103+0	588−12	722−3	490−2	860−2
6. E.S.C.	Max.	229+1	154+2	482+0	700+6	410−2	820−2	355−1
	Min.	176+0	870+0	143+0	413+1	188−2	599−2	840−2

7. W.S.C.	Max.	$732+0$	$104+2$	$880+0$	$176+2$	$539-2$	$880-2$	$416-0$
	Min.	$239-4$	$140-4$	$152+0$	$679-25$	$222-3$	$442-2$	$125-1$
8. M.	Max.	$862+0$	$431+1$	$641+0$	$108+2$	$190-2$	$105-1$	$330+1$
	Min.	$539-10$	$200-11$	$252+0$	$342-31$	$141-4$	$381-2$	$216-1$
9. P.	Max.	$980+0$	$155+2$	$497+0$	$209+2$	$600-2$	$114-1$	$153+2$
	Min.	$800-14$	$117-14$	$209+0$	$580-27$	$557-5$	$328-2$	$362-1$

Note: $333+2$ is $333 \times 10^2 = 33{,}300$. Correspondingly $333+0$ is $333 \times 10^0 = 333$ and $333-2$ is $333 \times 10^{-2} = 3.33$.

theless, table 7.1 gives seven negative parameter values, i.e., for $\eta, \vartheta, \mu, \nu, \chi, \psi$ and ω.

For η and ϑ which are parameters in eq. (3.5) determining the development of regional capital stocks over time we tried to find a theoretical explanation of the negative values. This was done in chapter 6, paragraph 9–12. The explanation found was not very satisfactory. But even if it had been, it would have been questionable just to run the model using negative parameter values. Let us go back to chapter 6, paragraph 9 to see one of the reasons why. In this paragraph the rate of interest is drawn into the picture as something determined by the growth of capital. But in eq. (3.5) it is the rate of interest which determines the growth of capital. This inter-dependence should lead to a reformulation of the model, which we have not done.

In chapter 6, paragraph 25 we found a possible theoretical explanation of the negative ν-value, i.e., the decreasing returns to investment in education. We are, however, not very proud of this change of explanation.

The negative values for μ, χ, ψ and ω we did not even try to explain.

But after all, we have done the estimations. So we shall try to run the model.

3 The work was done at NEUCC, the Northern European University Computing Center in Copenhagen, in cooperation with Bjarne Andersson who wrote the computer programs given in appendix B below.

The status variables are the observed 1880-values of the Y's, the K's, the L's and the U's and the estimated 1880-values of the gammas and the E's. Computing the values of these six variables and those of the income per capita for each year of the period 1880–1950 gives us about 4.900 computed values. Instead of printing the figures we shall present our results in diagrams drawn by the computer. If we have observations of the variables for 1900, 1919–21 and maybe also 1949–51, these observations are used in the diagrams instead of the computed values. This should make it rather easy to get an impression of the differences between observed and computed values.

4   The results are shown in fig. 7.1. They are very discouraging. To run our full model using our preliminary "estimates" of the parameters does not seem to make sense.

So, let us try with the simplified one.

CHAPTER 8

Alternative 2

1   In this chapter we shall run the simplified Cobb–Douglas model given in chapter 6 paragraph 31. Doing so, we shall use the preliminary "estimates" of the betas, deltas and gammas and the values of the exponential parameters presented as alternative 2. For convenience the latter are given in table 8.1.

TABLE 8.1

The estimated values of the exponential parameters.

Code*		Parameter	Value
P	1	Γ	0.0327
P	2	ζ	0.0377
P	3	η	−0.1370
P	5	Θ	0.0177
P	6	κ	0.0261
P	7	λ	0.0523
P	9	Λ	0.0106
P	10	κ	−0.0170

*The code refers to the computer
programme in appendix B.

2   The theory behind the simplified model demands all exponential parameter values to be positive, except the value of κ which is assumed to be negative. Therefore, table 8.1 looks much more satisfactory than table 7.1. The negative η-value is the only deviation from the assumptions. It is serious enough

Alternative 2

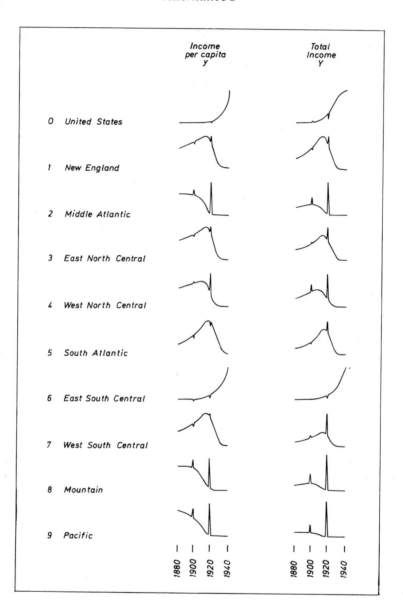

Fig. 8.1.

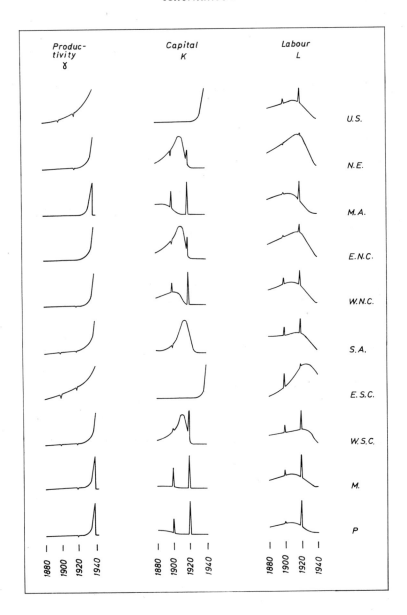

Fig. 8.1 (*continued*).

but we feel somewhat more comfortable than we did last time we started running a model.

3 The results given in fig. 8.1 show that we had little reason for feeling so. They are very discouraging indeed. Alternative 2

TABLE 8.2

Maximum and minimum values of the variables in fig. 8.1.

		y	Y	γ	K	L
		1929 dollars	Millions of 1929 dollars		Millions of 1929 dollars	Millions
0. U.S.	Max.	396 + 2	395 + 3	433 + 0	267 + 8	414 − 1
	Min.	330 + 0	151 + 2	114 + 0	750 + 2	380 − 2
1. N.E.	Max.	628 + 0	516 + 1	232 + 1	388 + 2	323 − 2
	Min.	167 − 5	623 − 6	133 + 0	385 − 27	142 − 3
2. M.A.	Max.	674 + 0	177 + 2	101 + 2	728 + 2	993 − 2
	Min.	000 + 0	000 + 0	000 + 0	000 + 0	000 + 0
3. E.N.C.	Max.	615 + 0	138 + 2	204 + 1	873 + 2	851 − 2
	Min.	165 − 5	126 − 5	111 + 0	894 − 26	290 − 3
4. W.N.C.	Max.	548 + 0	662 + 1	576 + 1	408 + 2	459 − 2
	Min.	110 − 8	735 − 10	960 − 1	356 − 40	254 − 4
5. S.A.	Max.	473 + 0	430 + 1	130 + 1	540 + 2	441 − 2
	Min.	599 − 3	563 − 3	940 − 1	112 − 18	357 − 3
6. E.S.C.	Max.	792 + 1	586 + 2	433 + 0	267 + 8	331 − 2
	Min.	176 + 0	870 + 0	127 + 0	413 + 1	188 − 2
7. W.S.C.	Max.	453 + 0	428 + 1	218 + 1	176 + 2	372 − 2
	Min.	131 − 3	590 − 4	144 + 0	604 − 26	171 − 3
8. M.	Max.	623 + 0	206 + 1	519 + 1	108 + 2	125 − 2
	Min.	000 + 0	000 + 0	000 + 0	000 + 0	000 + 0
9. P.	Max.	690 + 0	439 + 1	767 + 1	209 + 2	241 − 2
	Min.	000 + 0	000 + 0	000 + 0	000 + 0	000 + 0

Note: $333 + 2$ is $333 \times 10^2 = 33{,}300$. Correspondingly $333 + 0$ is $333 \times 10^0 = 333$ and $333 − 2$ is $333 \times 10^{-2} = 3.33$.

seems to be as poor as alternative 1. We may therefore ask:
why do we get such poor results and what can we do to get some
better ones?

4   Figs. 7.1 and 8.1 show that the models work far better in the
first half than in the second half of the period considered. The
explanation might be an accumulation of errors which after a
number of years becomes serious. We might get better results
by building in adjustment mechanisms correcting errors along
the road. We might also get better results by starting the runs in
1920, moving forwards to 1950 and backwards to 1880. Our
impression is, however, that the explanation of the poor results
has to be found in something more fundamental.

5   One possibility is the method of estimation. In chapter 6 we
did our estimates in a series of conventional partial multiple
regression analyses. Instead, we might have done a simultaneous estimation of all the exponential parameters of the model.
After the unhappy experience with the partial estimations we
did, in fact, such a simultaneous estimation. The result was even
worse than that of the partial ones. This supported the idea that
the crucial point was not the method of estimation but the data.

6   We have to realize that we can make no direct use of the
"estimates" produced in chapter 6. But the work has not been
done in vain. Chapter 9 will show why.

CHAPTER 9

A numerical example

1   In this chapter we shall return to our full CES model. We shall assume that we were right in demanding positive values for the exponential parameters and we shall try to run the model with assigned values for these parameters.

The assignment process comes very close to what sometimes is called "qualified guessing". It is a guess, but it is qualified because we shall have another look at our chapter 6 "estimates" before we assign the parameter values.

The values assigned are those given in table 9.1.

2   The results of the runs are shown in fig. 9.1. They leave room for improvement, but they are by no means discouraging and far better than those of chapters 7 and 8.

After all, it looks as if the model makes sense.

TABLE 9.1
The assigned values of the exponential variables.

Code*	Parameter	Value	Code*	Parameter	Value
P 1	Γ	0.0327	P 11	π	0.0025
P 2	ζ	0.0150	P 12	τ	0.0050
P 3	η	0.0050	P 13	Ξ	0.0089
P 4	ϑ	0.0025	P 14	υ	0.0050
P 5	Θ	0.0177	P 15	φ	0.0025
P 6	H	0.0150	P 16	χ	0.0025
P 7	λ	0.0200	P 17	Ω	0.0104
P 8	μ	0.0025	P 18	ψ	0.0025
P 9	Λ	0.0113	P 19	ω	0.0025
P 10	ν	0.0050			

*The code refers to the computer programme in appendix B.

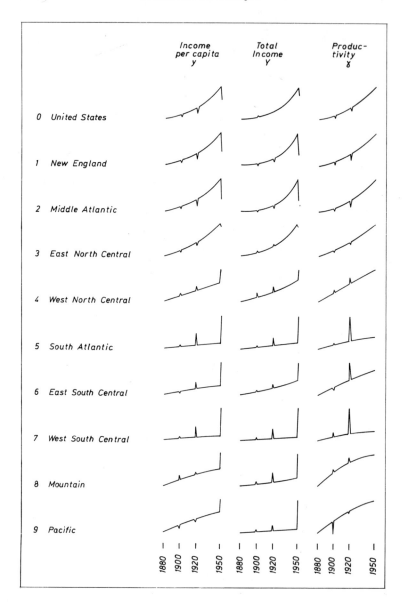

Fig. 9.1.

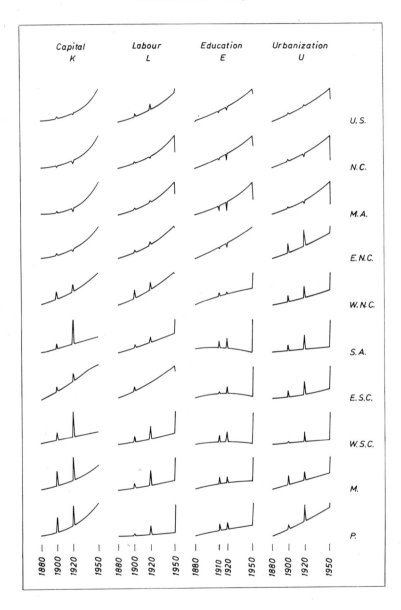

Fig. 9.1 (*continued*).

TABLE 9.2
Maximum and minimum values of the variables in fig. 9.1.

		y	Y	γ	K	L	E	U
		1929 dollars	Millions of 1929 dollars		Millions of 1929 dollars	Millions	Years of school completed	Percent
0. U.S.	Max.	$122+1$	$181+3$	$463+0$	$807+3$	$598-1$	$102-1$	$740-1$
	Min.	$331+0$	$151+2$	$151+0$	$750+2$	$173-1$	$510-2$	$280-1$
1. N.E.	Max.	$151+1$	$246+2$	$530+0$	$115+3$	$620-2$	$125-1$	$122+0$
	Min.	$410+0$	$169+1$	$175+0$	$861+1$	$157-2$	$520-2$	$524-1$
2. M.A.	Max.	$192+1$	$909+2$	$536+0$	$397+3$	$180-1$	$144-1$	$124+0$
	Min.	$444+0$	$481+1$	$154+0$	$234+2$	$412-2$	$540-2$	$492-1$
3. E.N.C.	Max.	$982+0$	$325+2$	$363+0$	$174+3$	$126-1$	$960-2$	$657-1$
	Min.	$366+0$	$348+1$	$157+0$	$187+2$	$362-2$	$510-2$	$275-1$
4. W.N.C.	Max.	$822+0$	$120+2$	$216+0$	$573+2$	$561-2$	$930-2$	$499-1$
	Min.	$323+0$	$171+1$	$130+0$	$922+1$	$201-2$	$520-2$	$182-1$
5. S.A.	Max.	$625+0$	$112+2$	$222+0$	$202+2$	$680-2$	$830-2$	$382-1$
	Min.	$149+0$	$877+0$	$103+0$	$444+1$	$223-2$	$523-2$	$860-2$
6. E.S.C.	Max.	$561+0$	$686+1$	$245+0$	$133+2$	$467-2$	$820-2$	$355-1$
	Min.	$176+0$	$870+0$	$143+0$	$413+1$	$188-2$	$600-2$	$840-2$

7. W.S.C.	Max.	732 + 0	104 + 2	292 + 0	176 + 2	539 − 2	880 − 2	530 − 1
	Min.	203 + 0	611 + 0	152 + 0	258 + 1	115 − 2	500 − 2	125 − 1
8. M.	Max.	862 + 0	431 + 1	312 + 0	108 + 2	190 − 2	105 − 1	488 − 1
	Min.	462 + 0	344 + 0	252 + 0	124 + 1	283 − 3	470 − 2	216 − 1
9. P.	Max.	980 + 0	155 + 2	264 + 0	216 + 2	600 − 2	114 − 1	629 − 1
	Min.	548 + 0	682 + 0	209 + 0	269 + 1	473 − 3	430 − 2	362 − 1

Note: $333 + 2$ is $333 \times 10^2 = 33{,}300$. Correspondingly $333 + 0$ is $333 \times 10^0 = 333$ and $333 - 2$ is $333 \times 10^{-2} = 3.33$.

CHAPTER 10

Conclusions

1   The most important conclusion of part three is that it probably makes sense to integrate into the model of part two basic
elements of the theories surveyed in part one.

2   If this is the case the model might be of some help in the
making of regional policies, i.a., because it can tell how a change
in a parameter might change regional economic developments.[1]

3   Much more empirical work is needed before a model like
ours should be relied upon for specific policy recommendations.

[1]Appendix A elaborates this point by showing how a change in the parameter
λ (determining labour response to regional differences in the wage rate) might
affect regional labour forces, capital stocks, productivities, levels of education,
degrees of urbanization and incomes per capita 2, 10 and 25 years ahead.

APPENDICES

λ-*Elasticities*

1   In this appendix we shall see how many percent a one percent change in the exponential variable λ might change regional incomes per capita, total incomes, productivities, capital stocks, labour forces, levels of education and degrees of urbanization over time.

This is done by running the full CES model using the table 9.1 assigned values of the exponential parameters except for λ which is changed from 0.200 to 0.202.

Fig. A.1 shows the difference in percent between the results of these runs and the results of the chapter 9 runs.

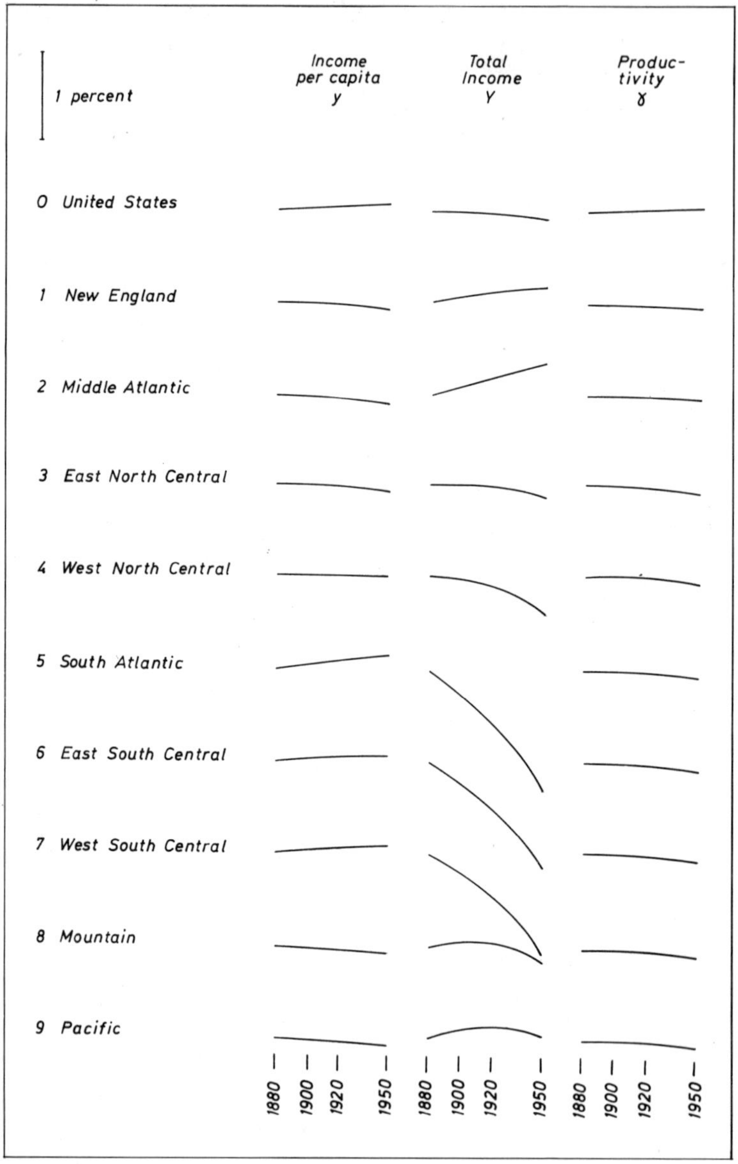
1 percent
Income per capita y
Total Income Y
Productivity γ
0 United States
1 New England
2 Middle Atlantic
3 East North Central
4 West North Central
5 South Atlantic
6 East South Central
7 West South Central
8 Mountain
9 Pacific
1880
1900
1920
1950

Fig. A.1.

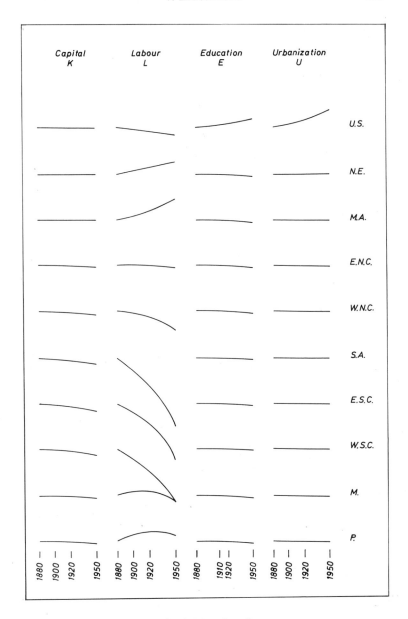

Fig. A.1 (*continued*).

The computer programs

BY BJARNE ANDERSSON

1 To facilitate the reading of the programs we shall start by presenting the following list of symbols:

$$B = \beta_i \quad (i = 1, 2, \ldots, 9)$$
$$D = \delta_i \quad (i = 1, 2, \ldots, 9)$$
$$P = \text{Vector of exponential parameters}$$
$$DIJ = d_{ij} \quad (i = 1, 2, \ldots, 9)\,(j = 1, 2, \ldots, 9)$$
$$A = a$$
$$Y = Y_i \quad (i = 1, 2, \ldots, 9)$$
$$LY = y_i \quad (i = 1, 2, \ldots, 9)$$
$$GA = \gamma_i \quad (i = 1, 2, \ldots, 9)$$
$$K = K_i \quad (i = 1, 2, \ldots, 9)$$
$$L = L_i \quad (i = 1, 2, \ldots, 9)$$
$$E = E_i \quad (i = 1, 2, \ldots, 9)$$
$$U = U_i \quad (i = 1, 2, \ldots, 9)$$
$$LR = r_i \quad (i = 1, 2, \ldots, 9)$$
$$V = {}_iV \quad (i = 1, 2, \ldots, 9)$$
$$W = w_i \quad (i = 1, 2, \ldots, 9)$$

If UI is added to the symbol of a variable, e.g. LY, the new symbol, LYUI, is used for a national variable, in this case the national income per capita.

2   Running the full model developed in chapter 3 we are using
the following computer program:

```
C
C          MAIN PROGRAM
C
           COMMON B,D,P,DIJ,A
           COMMON Y,LY,GA,K,L,E,U,T,N,TT
           COMMON LYUI,LR,LRUI,V,VUI,LW,LWUI,EUI,UUI
           INTEGER N,T,TT
           REAL E(10),D(10),P(20),DIJ(10,10),A
           REAL Y(100,10),LY(100,10),GA(100,10),K(100,10),
          4L(100,10),E(100,10),U(100,10)
           REAL LYUI,LR(10),LRUI,V(10),VUI,LW(10),LWUI,EUI,UUI
888        T=1
C
C
C    NVAR=ANTAL EXPONENTIELLE VARIABLE NR., MAX 20
C    ORDNINGEN AF DE EXP.VARIABLE = K-L-GA-E-U.
C
           CALL IND(IBIR,NEND,ILIM)
885        WRITE(6,20)
20         FORMAT(1H1)
           TT=1
99         IF(TT.GT.1)WRITE(6,50)RTID,TT
50         FORMAT(///1X,16HITERATIONSTID = ,F7.4,6H  SEK.,08H FOR T= ,I3)
           CALL BLOK6
           CALL TIME(JX)
           CALL BLOK3
C
C    T FREMSKRIVES I BLOK 45
C
           CALL BLOK45
           CALL TIME(JY)
           RTID=JY-JX
           RTID=RTID/60.
           TT=TT+1
           IF(TT.LE.NEND)GOTO 99
           CALL POLG(NEND)
           IBIR=IBIR-1
           IF(IBIR.GT.0)GOTO 888
           STOP
           END
```

3   In subroutine IND, given below, the following READ-
variables are used:

N = Number of regions.

NEND = Number of iterations.

IBIR = Maximum number of alternative runs.

NVAR = Number of exponential variables.

ILIM = READ-processing variable: the variable is a
three digit integer. The first digit which could be
either 1 or 0 determines whether or not values of
the exponential parameters should be read into
the computer. The second digit which could be
either 2 or 0 determines whether or not DIJ

should be read into the computer. The third digit which could be either 3 or 0 determines whether or not the status variables should be read into the computer. (A zero value means that no reading is done.)

INIT = If INIT ≠ 1 a new run will use the old status variables.

```
      SUBROUTINE  INC(IBIR,NEND,ILIM)
      COMMON  B,D,P,DIJ,A
      COMMON  Y,LY,GA,K,L,E,U,T,N,TT
      COMMON  LYUI,LR,LRUI,V,VUI,LW,LWUI,EUI,UUI
      REAL  B(10),D(10),P(20),DIJ(10,10),A
      REAL  Y(100,10),LY(100,10),GA(100,10),K(100,10),
     *L(100,10),E(100,10),U(100,10)
      REAL  LYUI,LR(10),LRUI,V(10),VUI,LW(10),LWUI,EUI,UUI
      INTEGER  N,T,TT
      REAL  AY(10),ALY(10),AGA(10),AK(10),AL(10),AE(10),AU(10)
      ILIM=123
      IF(ILIM.GE.100)
     *READ(5,1)N,NEND,NVAR,ILIM,INIT,A,IBIR
1     FORMAT(515,F5.4,I1)
      IF(ILIM.GE.100)
     *READ(5,30)(P(I),I=1,NVAR)
30    FORMAT(10F7.4)
      IF(ILIM.GE.120.OR.ILIM.GE.20.AND.ILIM.LE.23)GOTO 10
      GOTO 11
10    DO 2 I=1,N
2     READ(5,31)(DIJ(I,J),J=1,N)
31    FORMAT(16F5.1)
11    IF(ILIM.EQ.103.OR.ILIM.EQ.123.OR.ILIM.EQ.23.OR.ILIM.EQ.3)GOTO 12
      GOTO 13
12    DO 20 I=1,N
      READ(5,3)AY(I)           ,AGA(I),AK(I),AL(I),AE(I),AU(I),B(I),D(I)
3     FORMAT(4F10.3,2F5.1,2F7.6)
20    ALY(I)=(AY(I)*A)/AL(I)
13    IF(INIT.EQ.1)GOTO 220
      DO 22 I=1,N
      Y(T,I)=AY(I)
      LY(T,I)=ALY(I)
      GA(T,I)=AGA(I)
      K(T,I)=AK(I)
      L(T,I)=AL(I)
      E(T,I)=AE(I)
22    U(T,I)=AU(I)
220   WRITE(6,100)N,NEND,NVAR,ILIM,INIT,A
      WRITE(6,101)P
      WRITE(6,1122)
      DO 110 L1P=1,N
110   WRITE(6,102)(DIJ(L2P,L1P),L2P=1,N)
100   FORMAT(1H1,/13H  ANTAL REG.=,I2,22H  ANTAL  ITERATIONER =,I3//1X,
     *  7H NVAR =,I3,  7H ILIM =,I4,25H                 INIT =,I4,
     *5H  A= ,F6.4)
101   FORMAT(1H0,/35H  CHECK AF EXPONENTIELLE VARIABLE..//1X,
     *4(1X,5H  K  ),4(1X,5H  L  ),4(1X,5H GA  ),4(1X,5H  E  ),
     *3(1X,5H  U  )/(1X,10F9.4))
102   FORMAT(1X,14F9.1)
1122  FORMAT(1H0,/1X,18H  AFSTANDSMATRICE..////)
      DO 7777 IR=1,N
      IZ=IR-1
7777  WRITE(6,7776) B(IR),D(IR),IZ
7776  FORMAT(91X,F9.6,3H*E*,F9.6,3H*D*,I2)
      RETURN
      END
```

```
SUBROUTINE BLCK6
COMMON B,D,P,DIJ,A
COMMON Y,LY,GA,K,L,E,U,T,N,TT
COMMON LYUI,LR,LRUI,V,VUI,LW,LWUI,EUI,UUI
REAL B(10),D(10),P(20),DIJ(10,10),A
REAL Y(100,10),LY(100,10),GA(100,10),K(100,10),
*L(100,10),E(100,10),U(100,10)
REAL LYUI,LR(10),LRUI,V(10),VUI,LW(10),LWUI,EUI,UUI
INTEGER T,N,TT
WRITE(6,10)TT
10      FORMAT(       1X,6HFOR T=,I3,2X,27HFAAS FOLGENDE RESULTATER...)
WRITE(6,1)
1       FORMAT(//1X,6X,1HY,15X,2HLY,14X,2HGA,14X,1HK,15X,1HL,15X,
*1HE,15X,1HU,14X,8HREG. NC.)
DO 2 I=1,N
IXV=I-1
2       WRITE(6,3)Y(T,I),LY(T,I),GA(T,I),K(T,I),L(T,I),E(T,I),U(T,I),IXV
3       FORMAT(7(1X,E15.7),3X,I2)
RETURN
END
```

```
      SUBROUTINE BLOK3
      COMMON B,D,P,DIJ,A
      COMMON Y,LY,GA,K,L,E,U,T,N,TT
      COMMON LYUI,LR,LRUI,V,VUI,LW,LWUI,EUI,UUI
      COMMON KV1,KV2,KV3,KV4,KV5,KV6
      REAL B(10),D(10),P(20),DIJ(10,10),A
      REAL Y(100,10),LY(100,10),GA(100,10),K(100,10),
     *L(100,10),E(100,10),U(100,10)
      REAL LYUI,LR(10),LRUI,V(10),VUI,LW(10),LWUI,EUI,UUI
      REAL KV1(10),KV2(10),KV3(10),KV4(10),KV5(10),KV6(10)
      INTEGER T,N,TT
10    FORMAT(8E16.7)
      SU1=0.
      SU2=0.
      SU3=0.
      SU4=0.
      SU6=0.
      SU7=0.
      SU8=0.
      SU9=0.
      SU11=0.
      LYUI=Y(T,1)/(L(T,1)/A)
      DO 2 I=2,N
      KV1(I)=LY(T,I)/LYUI
      ALFA=(-1./B(I))*GA(T,I)*( D(I)*K(T,I)**(-B(I))+(1.-D(I))*
     *L(T,I)**(-B(I))) **(-(1.+B(I))/B(I))
      LR( I)=ALFA*D(I)*(-B(I))*K(T,I)**(-1.-B(I))
      LW( I)=ALFA*(1.-D(I))*(-B(I))*L(T,I)**(-1.-B(I))
      IF(T.EQ.1.AND.I.LE.2)
     *WRITE(6,10)KV1(I),ALFA,LR(I),LW(I),SU3,SU4,SU7,SU8
2     CONTINUE
      I=1
      ALFA=(-1./B(I))*GA(T,I)*( D(I)*K(T,I)**(-B(I))+(1.-D(I))*
     *L(T,I)**(-B(I))) **(-(1.+B(I))/B(I))
      LRUI  = ALFA*D(I)*(-B(I))*K(T,I)**(-1.-B(I))
      LWUI  =ALFA*(1.-D(I))*(-B(I))*L(T,I)**(-1.-B(I))
      DO 3 I=2,N
      SU5=0.
      KV2(I)=LR( I)/LRUI
      KV4(I)=LW( I)/LWUI
      DO 4 J=2,N
4     SU5=SU5+Y(T,J)/DIJ(I,J)
      V( I)=SU5
      SU6=SU6+V(I)
30    IF(T.EQ.1.AND.I.LE.2)
     *WRITE(6,10)KV2(I),KV4(I),V(I),SU6
3     CONTINUE
      VUI=SU6/(FLOAT(N)-1.)
      DO 5 I=2,N
5     KV3(I)=V( I)/VUI
      EUI=E(T,1)
      UUI=U(T,1)
      DO 6 I=2,N
      KV5(I)=E(T,I)/EUI
      KV6(I)=U(T,I)/UUI
6     CONTINUE
      RETURN
      END
```

```
      SUBROUTINE BLOK45
      COMMON B,D,P,CIJ,A
      COMMON Y,LY,GA,K,L,E,U,T,N,TT
      COMMON LYUI,LR,LRUI,V,VUI,LW,LWUI,EUI,UUI
      COMMON KV1,KV2,KV3,KV4,KV5,KV6
      REAL B(10),D(10),P(20),CIJ(10,10),A
      REAL Y(100,10),LY(100,10),GA(100,10),K(100,10),
     *L(100,10),E(100,10),U(100,10)
      REAL LYUI,LR(10),LRUI,V(10),VUI,LW(10),LWUI,EUI,UUI
      REAL KV1(10),KV2(10),KV3(10),KV4(10),KV5(10),KV6(10)
      INTEGER T,N,TT
      DO 1 I=2,N
      K(T+1,I)= K(T,I)*EXP(P( 1))*KV1(I)**P( 2)*KV2(I)**P( 3)
     **KV3(I)**P(4)
      L(T+1,I)=L(T,I)*EXP(P(5))* (1./KV1(I)    )**P(6) *KV4(I)**P(7)
     **KV3(I)**P(8)
      GA(T+1,I)=GA(T,I)*EXP(P(9))*KV5(I)**P(10)*KV6(I)**P(11)
     **KV3(I)**P(12)
      E(T+1,I)=E(T,I)*EXP(P(13))*KV1(I)**P(14)*KV6(I)**P(15)
     **KV3(I)**P(16)
      U(T+1,I)=U(T,I)*EXP(P(17))*KV1(I)**P(18)*KV3(I)**P(19)
      Y(T+1,I)=GA(T+1,I)*(D(I)*K(T+1,T)**(-B(I))+(1.-D(I)))
     **L(T+1,I)**(-B(I)))**(-1./B(I))
      LY(T+1,I)=Y(T+1,I)/(L(T+1,I)/A)
1     CONTINUE
      SUY=0.
      SUL=0.
      SUK=0.
      DO 2 I=2,N
      SUY=SUY+Y(T+1,I)
      SUK=SUK+K(T+1,I)
2     SUL=SUL+L(T+1,I)
      WRITE(6,10)SUY
10    FORMAT(10X,E16.7)
      K(T+1,1)=SUK
      L(T+1,1)=SUL
      RGA=0.
      RE=0.
      RU=0.
      DO 3 I=2,N
      RGA=RGA+GA(T+1,I)*Y(T+1,I)
      RE=RE+E(T+1,I)*L(T+1,I)
3     RU=RU+U(T+1,I)*L(T+1,I)
      GA(T+1,1)=RGA/SUY
      E(T+1,1)=RE/L(T+1,1)
      U(T+1,1)=RU/L(T+1,1)
      Y(T+1,1)=GA(T+1,1)*(D(1)*K(T+1,1)**(-B(1))+(1.-D(1))
     **L(T+1,1)**(-B(1)))**(-1./B(1))
      LY(T+1,1)=Y(T+1,1)/(L(T+1,1)/A)
      T=T+1
      RETURN
      END
```

4 Drawing the curves of fig. 7.1 we use the following plot-routine (POLO) in which we read in the values of the relevant variables in 1900, 1920 and 1950.

```
      SUBROUTINE POLO(NE)
      COMMON B,D,P,DIJ,A
      COMMON Y,LY,GA,K,L,E,U,T,N,TT
      COMMON LYUI,LR,LRUI,V,VUI,LW,LWLT,EUI,UUI
      INTEGER N,T,TT
      REAL B(10),D(10),P(20),DIJ(10,10),A
      REAL Y(100,10),LY(100,10),GA(100,10),K(100,10),
     *L(100,10),E(100,10),J(100,10)
      REAL LYUI,LR(10),LRUI,V(10),VUI,LW(10),LWUI,EUI,UUI
      DIMENSION            VAN(7)       ,YP(100,10,7),YR(102),TA(102)
      DATA VAN/2H  Y,2HLY,2HGA,2H  K,2H  L,2H  E,2H  U/
      EQUIVALENCE (YP(1,1,1),Y(1,1)),(YP(1,1,2),LY(1,1)),
     *(YP(1,1,3),GA(1,1)),(YP(1,1,4),K(1,1)),
     *(YP(1,1,5),L(1,1)),(YP(1,1,6),E(1,1)),(YP(1,1,7),U(1,1))
      IE1=NE
    1 FORMAT(3F10.2)
      END=NE
      IE2=NE+1
      IE3=NE+2
      DO 4 IX=1,10
      DO 3 IXX=1,NE
      YP(IXX,IX,1) =    Y(IXX,IX)
      YP(IXX,IX,2) =   LY(IXX,IX)
      YP(IXX,IX,3) =   GA(IXX,IX)
      YP(IXX,IX,4) =    K(IXX,IX)
      YP(IXX,IX,5) =    L(IXX,IX)
      YP(IXX,IX,6) =    E(IXX,IX)
    3 YP(IXX,IX,7) =    U(IXX,IX)
      DO 2 I=1,10
      READ(5,1) YP(20,I,1),YP(40,I,1),YP(70,I,1)
      READ(5,1) YP(20,I,3),YP(40,I,3)
      READ(5,1) YP(20,I,4),YP(40,I,4)
      READ(5,1) YP(20,I,5),YP(40,I,5),YP(70,I,5)
      READ(5,1) YP(20,I,6),YP(40,I,6),YP(70,I,6)
      READ(5,1) YP(20,I,7),YP(40,I,7),YP(70,I,7)
      YP(20,I,2)=YP(20,I,1)/(YP(20,I,5)/A)
      YP(40,I,2)=YP(40,I,1)/(YP(40,I,5)/A)
      YP(70,I,2)=YP(70,I,1)/(YP(70,I,5)/A)
    2 CONTINUE
      CALL PARALF(B,0,0,0)
      HJ=5.
      KIEPU=1
      EK=FLOAT(IE1-1)/8.
      PEK = EK+2.
      PEKK=PEK+1.
      TEK1=(EK-1.7)/2.
```

```
      DO 4 J=1,7
      DO 5 I= 1,N
      ZY = I-1
      YMIN=2.##30
      YMAX=-2.##29
      DO 6 M=1,IE1
      YR(M)=YP(M,I,J)
      IF(YR(M).GT.YMAX)YMAX=YR(N)
      IF(YR(M).LT.YMIN)YMIN=YR(N)
      TA(M) =M
6     CONTINUE
      VANAV = VAN(J)
      DIFY=YMAX-YMIN
      DIFX=TA(IE1)-TA(1)
      YMAL=(HJ-.25)/DIFY
      XMAL=EK/DIFX
      YNULP=YMIN-.25/YMAL
      XNULP=TA(1)
      CALL KURVE(TA,YR,IE1,KTEPU,XMAL,YMAL,XNULP,YNULP,-1,11,0.01)
      XT2=XNULP+0.5/XMAL
      YT2=YNULP+1.0/YMAL
      CALL SYMBOL(.5,4.05,.18,6HYAXMS=,0.,6)
      CALL NUMBER(1.6,4.05,.18,YSTOK,0.,2)
      CALL SYMBOL(.5,4.45,.3,VANAV,0.,3)
      CALL NUMBER(.5,4.95,.3,ZY,0.,-1)
      CALL SYMBOL(.5,4.95,.3,4HREG=,0.,4)
      CALL AXE(0.,0.,EK,0.,XNULP,XT2,XSTOK,,12,-1.0,0.,-1.,1.)
      CALL SYMBOL(TEK1,-.7,.2,5HTIO I AA6,0.,9)
2222  CALL AXE(0.,0.,HJ,90.,YNULP,YT2,YSTOK,,13,1.,1.,3,1.,1.)
      GOTO(10,11,10,12,10,10,13,10,10,14),I
10    CALL PARALF(0.,7.)
      GOTO 5
11    CALL PARALF(PEK,-7.)
      GOTO 5
12    CALL PARALF(-PEK,17.)
      GOTO 5
13    CALL PARALF(PEK,-14.)
      GOTO 5
14    CALL PARALF(PEKK,-38.)
5     CONTINUE
4     CONTINUE
      RETURN
      END
```

5 Running the simplified Cobb–Douglas model developed in chapter 6, paragraph 31, we shall use the same programs changing only BLOK 3 and BLOK 45.

The new BLOK 3 is as follows:

```
      SUBROUTINE BLOK3
      COMMON B,D,P,DIJ,A
      COMMON Y,LY,GA,K,L,E,U,T,N,TT
      COMMON LYUI,LR,LRUI,V,VUI,LW,LWUI,EUI,UUI
      COMMON KV1,KV2,KV3,KV4,KV5,KV6
      REAL B(10),D(10),P(20),DIJ(10,10),A
      REAL Y(100,10),LY(100,10),GA(100,10),K(100,10),
     *L(100,10),E(100,10),U(100,10)
      REAL LYUI,LR(10),LRUI,V(10),VUI,LW(10),LWUI,EUI,UUI
      REAL KV1(10),KV2(10),KV3(10),KV4(10),KV5(10),KV6(10)
      INTEGER T,N,TT
   10 FORMAT(8E16.7)
      SU1=0.
      SU2=0.
      SU3=0.
      SU4=0.
      SU6=0.
      SU7=0.
      SU8=0.
      SU9=0.
      SU11=0.
      LYUI=Y(T,1)/(L(T,1)/A)
      DO 2 I=2,N
      KV1(I)=LY(T,I)/LYUI
      LR(I)=GA(T,I)*L(T,I)**(1.-D(I))*D(I)*K(T,I)**(D(I)-1.)
      LW(I)=GA(T,I)*K(T,I)**D(I)*(1.-D(I))*L(T,I)**(-D(I))
      IF(T.EQ.1.AND.I.LE.2)
     *WRITE(6,10)KV1(I),ALFA,LR(I),LW(I),SU3,SU4,SU7,SU8
    2 CONTINUE
      LRUI=GA(T,1)*L(T,1)**(1.-D(1))*D(1)*K(T,1)**(D(1)-1.)
      LWUI=GA(T,1)*K(T,1)**D(1)*(1.-D(1))*L(T,1)**(-D(1))
      DO 3 I=2,N
      SU5=0.
      KV2(I)=LR(  I)/LRUI
      KV4(I)=LW(  I)/LWUI
      IF(I.GT.2)GOTO 3
   30 IF(T.EQ.1.AND.I.LE.2)
     *WRITE(6,10)KV2(I),KV4(I),V(I),SU6
    3 CONTINUE
      RETURN
      END
```

Appendix B

The new **BLOK** 45 is as follows:

```
SUBROUTINE BLOK45
COMMON B,D,P,DIJ,A
COMMON Y,LY,GA,K,L,E,U,T,N,TT
COMMON LYUI,LR,LRUI,V,VUI,LW,LWUI,EUI,UUI
COMMON KV1,KV2,KV3,KV4,KV5,KV6
REAL B(10),D(10),P(20),DIJ(10,10),A
REAL Y(100,10),LY(100,10),GA(100,10),K(100,10),
*L(100,10),E(100,10),U(100,10)
REAL LYUI,LR(10),LRUI,V(10),VUI,LW(10),LWUI,EUI,UUI
REAL KV1(10),KV2(10),KV3(10),KV4(10),KV5(10),KV6(10)
INTEGER T,N,TT
DO 1 I=2,N
 K(T+1,I)= K(T,I)*EXP(P( 1))*KV1(I)**P( 2)*KV2(I)**P( 3)
 L(T+1,I)=L(T,I)*EXP(P(8))* (1./KV1(I)  )**P(6) *KV4(I)**P(7)
GA(T+1,I)=GA(T,I)*EXP(P(9))*KV1(I)**P(10)
Y(T+1,I)=GA(T+1,I)*K(T+1,I)**D(I)*L(T+1,I)**(1.-D(I))
LY(T+1,I)=Y(T+1,I)/(L(T+1,I)/A)
1   CONTINUE
SUY=0.
SUL=0.
SUK=0.
DO 2 I=2,N
SUY=SUY+Y(T+1,I)
SUK=SUK+K(T+1,I)
2   SUL=SUL+L(T+1,I)
WRITE(6,10)SUY
10  FORMAT(10X,E16.7)
K(T+1,1)=SUK
L(T+1,1)=SUL
RGA=0.
DO 3 I=2,N
3   RGA=RGA+GA(T+1,I)*Y(T+1,I)
GA(T+1,1)=RGA/SUY
Y(T+1,1)=GA(T+1,1)*K(T+1,1)**D(I)*L(T+1,1)**(1.-D(I))
LY(T+1,1)=Y(T+1,1)/(L(T+1,1)/A)
T=T+1
RETURN
END
```

APPENDIX C

Sensitivity analysis on a hybrid computer

BY BJARNE ANDERSSON AND ERLING OLSEN

1   This appendix is a post scriptum. When the manuscript was accepted as a doctoral dissertation by the university of Copenhagen, the author took a day off at the research establishment Risø of the Danish Atomic Energy Commission. Together with fellow-members of the Commission he inspected the new toys of the research staff. The most fascinating one was a hybrid computer system EAI 680/PDP8 with a display screen. The computer was used for simulation of biological as well as mechanical systems and the effects of continuous parameter variations were visualized on the display screen.

2   The author got the idea that the computer should be used for simulation of social systems also. He asked for permission to try his own model on the hybrid computer. The Commission kindly gave this permission and Mr. K. Søe Højberg and Mr. Christian Suusgaard promised to help him. The Danish State Social Science Research Council helped with an additional grant which made it possible to re-employ Mr. Bjarne Andersson.

The simplified model

3   There we were again. Our purpose was to show how such a computer could be used in the social sciences. Much insight could be gained if the effects of continuous parameter variations in a model could be visualized on the computer's display screen. But we had to simplify our model.

200 *Appendix C*

The first reason is that it would make our task easier if we could limit the use of the display screen. Therefore, we decided to construct an index, I^t, for the regional inequality of income at time t. This was done in a rather conventional way by formula (A.C.1).

$$I^t = \sum_{i=1}^{n} \left[\frac{Y_i^t - Y^t L_i^t / L^t}{Y^t L_i^t / L^t} \right]^2.$$
(A.C.1)

I^t is zero if the income per member of the labour force is the same in all regions.

The I^t curve for t-values between 1880 and 1950 are shown on the computer's display screen (cf. fig. A.C.2). Later, we shall see how this curve is changed by parameter variations in the model.

4 Secondly, we had to simplify the model because the digital component of the hybrid computer of Risø is not the IBM 7094/I-360/30 which we used at the Northern Europe University Computing Center.

We decided to substitute the Cobb–Douglas production function of eq. (A.C.2) for the CES-function of eq. (3.1).

$$Y_i^t = \gamma_i^t (K_i^t)^\delta (L_i^t)^{1-\delta}.$$
(A.C.2)

The values of γ_i^t were determined as follows:
Firstly the values of Λ_i for $i = 1, 2, \ldots, n$ were estimated using eq. (A.C.3) and the data of table 6.18.

$$e^{40\Lambda_i} = \frac{\gamma_i^{1919-21}}{\gamma_i^{1880}}.$$
(A.C.3)

Then the values of γ_i^t were determined by the values of γ_i^{1880} given by table 6.18 and eq. (A.C.4).

$$\gamma_i^{t+1} = e^{\Lambda_i} \gamma_i^t.$$
(A.C.4)

The value of δ is 0.242 or the one given by table 6.2.

5 Eq. (A.C.5) substituting eq. (3.5) shows the growth of the regional capital stocks.

$$K_i^{t+1} = K_i^t e^{\Gamma} \left(\frac{r_i^t}{r^t}\right)^{\eta} \left(\frac{_iV^t}{V^t}\right)^{\vartheta}. \qquad \text{(A.C.5)}$$

The value of Γ is 0.0327 or the estimate of chapter 6, paragraph 5.

Eq. (A.C.6) substituting eq. (3.12) shows the growth of the regional labour forces

$$L_i^{t+1} = L_i^t e^{\Theta} \left(\frac{w_i^t}{w^t}\right)^{\lambda} \left(\frac{_iV^t}{V^t}\right)^{\mu}. \qquad \text{(A.C.6)}$$

The value of Θ is 0.0177 or the estimate of chapter 6, paragraph 15.

The simplified program

6 To save computer time we used five small tricks.

Firstly, we transformed the equations to logarithms. Eq. (A.C.2), for example, was given the form:

$$\ln Y_i^t = \ln \gamma_i^t + \delta \ln K_i^t + (1-\delta) \ln L_i^t. \qquad \text{(A.C.7)}$$

Secondly, we transformed the values of the natural logarithms to integers using the formula:

$$\ln (\text{argument}) \; 100. \rightarrow \text{integer result.} \qquad \text{(A.C.8)}$$

The natural logarithm of 10 or $\ln(10.0)$, for example, was transformed to the integer 230. Thirdly, we transformed 151 relevant values of e^x, $(x = 5.5, 5.6, \ldots, 20.4, 20.5)$, to real constants which were placed as an array, EP(I), in the core memory of the PDP8.

Fourthly, we substituted seven ten-year periods for the seventy one-year periods from 1880 to 1950.

Fifthly, we made a special program loading procedure profiting from the disc facilities of the PDP8 system.

7 These operations reduced both the time and the accuracy of the computations.

Table A.C.1 gives an impression of the computer time saved by the transformations.

TABLE A.C.1
PDP8 computer times for the
FORTRAN system used.

Operation	Seconds	
$A = 1500. + 500.$	1	M
$A = 1500. * 500.$	3	$\cdot$ M
$A = 1500. /500.$	4.5	M
$A = 1500. ** 3.1$	100	M
$A = ELOG (10.)$	28	M
$A = EXP (10.)$	54	M
$A = 1500.$	0.5	M
$I = 1500.$	0.7	M
$I = 1500. + 500.$	~ 10	μ

Note: All operations of reals are software operations.

The loss of accuracy was indicated by parallel runs of the model on the Risø and the NEUCC computer systems. The indications did not discourage us.

8 The block diagram of fig. A.C.1 shows Risø's EAI 680/ PDP8 hybrid computer system.[1] It also shows how the analog component of the system was programmed.

[1]See also K. Søe Højberg, *Risø hybrid computer, hardware and software*, Danish Atomic Energy Commission, Research Establishment Risø, Risø-M-1272, DK-4000 Roskilde, July 1970.

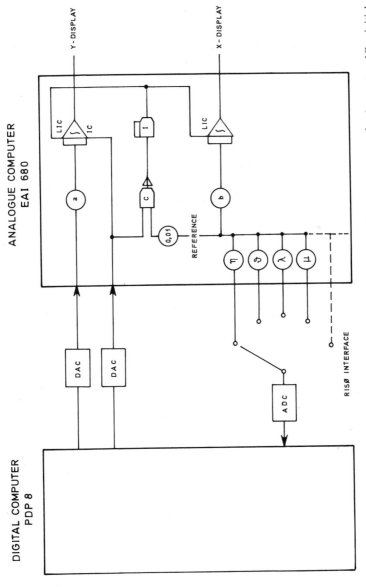

Fig. A.C.1. DAC = digital to analogue converter; ADC = analogue to digital converter; $\int$ = integrator; IC = initial condition; LIC = logic IC/operate control; C = comparator; I = impulse generator.

The digital component of the hybrid computer was pro-grammed as follows:

```
C                         MAIN PROGRAM
C
      COMMON IX,IDI,IP1,IP4,D,ID,IDI,IY,IAK,IAL,IG,IA,EP
      DIMENSION IX(65),IDI(9,9),IAK(3,10),IAL(3,10),EP(151)
      DIMENSION IA(10),IY(3,10),IG(3,10)
      I=0
      DO 5 J=550,2040,10
      I=I+1
      RR=FLOAT(J)/100.
5     EP(I)=EXP(RR)
      EP(151)=EXP(20.50)
      D=.242
      READ(1,10)ID
      DO 1 I=1,10
      READ(1,10)IY(1,I)
      READ(1,10)IAK(1,I)
      READ(1,10)IAL(1,I)
      READ(1,10)IG(1,I)
1     READ(1,10)IA(I)
      DO 2 I=1,9
      DO 2 J=1,9
      READ(1,10)IDI(I,J)
2     IDI(J,I)=IDI(I,J)
      READ(1,10)IP1
      READ(1,10)IP4
      READ(1,10)IDI
      DO 4 I=1,10
      II=I*10
      WRITE(1,13)EP(II)
      WRITE(1,14)IG(1,I),IA(I)
4     WRITE(1,12)IDI(I,I),IY(1,I),IAK(1,I),IAL(1,I)
      PAUSE 1
10    FORMAT(I5)
13    FORMAT(E11.5)
12    FORMAT(7X,I7,3X,I5,3X,I5,3X,I5)
14    FORMAT(2X,I5,3X,I5)
      END
```

```
C          PROCESS
C
           COMMON IX,IDI,IP1,IP4,D,ID,ID1,IY,IAK,IAL,IG,IA,EP
           DIMENSION IX(65),ID1(9,9),IVK1(10),IVK3(10),VK2(10)
           DIMENSION Y(10),IY(3,10),IAK(3,10),IAL(3,10),IG(3,10),IA(10)
           DIMENSION IVK2(10),RX(2),EP(151)
           D1=0.758
1004       MX=1
           RX(1)=0.97545
           IT=0
1000       IF(IT-10)60,61,60
61         CALL DAC(6,0)
           CALL DAC(6,975)
60         DO 40 I=1,10
           IY(2,I)=IY(MX,I)
           IAK(2,I)=IAK(MX,I)
           IAL(2,I)=IAL(MX,I)
40         IG(2,I)=IG(MX,I)
           RX(2)=0.
           IT=IT+10
           P5=IADC(0)
           P5=P5/2047.
           P6=IADC(1)
           P6=P6/2047.
           P2=IADC(2)
           P2=P2/2047.
           P3=IADC(3)
           P3=P3/2047.
           DO 7 I=1,10
           IL=FLOAT(IAL(2,I))*D1
           IK=-FLOAT(IAK(2,I))*D1
           JK=FLOAT(IAK(2,I))*D
           JL=-FLOAT(IAL(2,I))*D
           IVK1(I)=IG(2,I)+IL+ID+IK
           IVK3(I)=IG(2,I)+JK+ID1+JL
7          VK2(I)=0.
           DO 8 I=2,10
           IVK1(I)=IVK1(I)-IVK1(1)
           IVK3(I)=IVK3(I)-IVK3(1)
           DO 87 J=2,10
87         VK2(I)=VK2(I)+EP((IY(2,J)-IDI(I-1,J-1))/10+1)/20.09
8          VK2(I)=VK2(I)+VK2(I)
           VK2(I)=VK2(I)/9.
           IVK2(I)=ELOG(VK2(I))*100.
           DO 88 I=2,10
           IVK2(I)=ELOG(VK2(I))*100.
88         IVK2(I)=IVK2(I)-IVK2(1)
```

```
A1=0.
A2=0.
DO 9 I=2,10
IV1=FLOAT(IVK1(I))*P2
IV2=FLOAT(IVK2(I))*P3
IV3=FLOAT(IVK3(I))*P5
IV4=FLOAT(IVK2(I))*P6
IAK(3,I)=IAK(2,I)+IP1+IV1+IV2
IAL(3,I)=IAL(2,I)+IP4+IV3+IV4
A1=A1+EP((IAK(3,I)-545)/10+1)
IPL=(IAL(3,I)+250)/10+1
REL=IREM(XX)
9     A2=A2+(EP(IPL)+(EP(IPL+1)-EP(IPL))/10.*REL)/2981.
IAK(3,I)=ELOG(A1)*100.
IAL(3,I)=ELOG(A2)*100.
DO 20 I=1,10
IG(3,I)=IG(2,I)+IA(I)
IK=FLOAT(IAK(3,I))*D
IL=FLOAT(IAL(3,I))*D1
IY(3,I)=IG(3,I)+IK+IL
IPY=(IY(3,I)-550)/10+1
REY=IREM(XX)
20    Y(I)=EP(IPY)+(EP(IPY+1)-EP(IPY))/10.*REY
DO 21 I=2,10
IR=IY(3,I)+IAL(3,I)-IAL(3,I)
IPR=(IR-550)/10+1
RRR=IREM(XX)
RR=EP(IPR)+(EP(IPR+1)-EP(IPR))/10.*RRR
21    RX(2)=RX(2)+(Y(I)-RR)/RR*(Y(I)-RR)/RR
IDX=(RX(2)-RX(1))*2000.
CALL DAC(7,IDX)
M=RX(2)*1000.
CALL DAC(0,M)
MX=3
RX(1)=RX(2)
IF(IT-70)1000,1004,1004
END
```

Running the model

9 Fig. A.C.2 is a photograph of the computer's display screen showing I^t for $1880 \leqslant t \leqslant 1950$. The initial value, I^{1880}, is 0.975. The horizontal line indicates the zero value of I^t. It is assumed that $\eta = \vartheta = \lambda = \mu = 0$. The development over time of I^t can only be explained by the given changes over time in the values of the regional efficiency parameters.

10 We now want to see how sensitive the I^t curve is to variations in η. This parameter indicates the speed of capital movements from regions with relatively low interest rates to regions

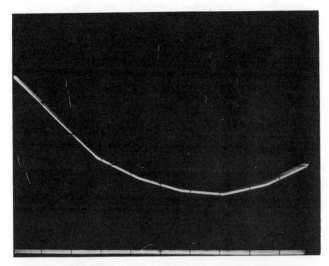

Fig. A.C.2. $\eta = \vartheta = \lambda = \mu = 0$.

with relatively high interest rates. Fig. A.C.3 shows I^t curves for six values of η, given $\vartheta = \lambda = \mu = 0$. The I^t curve moves

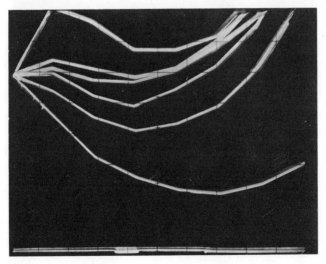

Fig. A.C.3. $\vartheta = \lambda = \mu = 0$; $\eta = 0.00, 0.25, 0.40, 0.50, 0.60$ and 1.00.

Appendix C

up in the diagram as the value of η increases. The regional distribution of income will be more unequal the faster capital moves from regions with low interest to regions with high interest rates. This absurd result can only be explained by the assumptions about the development over time of the regional efficiency parameters.

11 Our next step is to fix the value of η to 0.05 and to vary the value of ϑ. This parameter indicates the relative speed of capital movements in and out of regions with different levels of general interaction with the rest of the nation. Fig. A.C.4 shows I^t curves for four values of ϑ, given $\eta = 0.05$ and $\lambda = \mu = 0$.

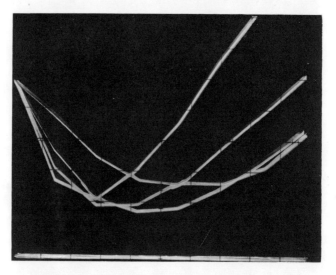

Fig. A.C.4. $\lambda = \mu = 0$; $\eta = 0.05$; $\vartheta = 0.00, 0.25, 0.40$ and 0.60.

The I^t curve moves left in the diagram as the value of ϑ increases. To some extent we could say that an increase in the value of ϑ has an effect comparable to that of an increase in the value of η.

12 Turning to the movements of labour, we shall see how sensitive the I^t curve is to changes in λ. Fig. A.C.5 shows I^t curves for three values of λ, given that $\eta = \vartheta = \mu = 0$. The

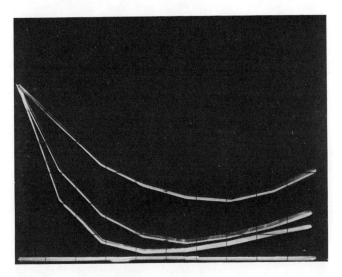

Fig. A.C.5. $\eta = \vartheta = \mu = 0$; $\lambda = 0.00, 0.50$ and 1.00.

I^t curve moves down in the diagram as the value of λ increases. The regional distribution of income becomes more equal the faster labour moves from regions with relatively low wages to regions with relatively high wages.

13 Fig. A.C.6 shows I^t curves for four values of μ, given $\lambda = 0.17$ and $\eta = \vartheta = 0$. The I^t curve moves up in the diagram as the value of μ increases. To explain this result we have to return to the assumptions about the growth in productivities.

14 Fig. A.C.7 shows the sensitivity of the I^t curve to variations in both η and ϑ. The curve moves up in the diagram as the values of η and ϑ increase.

Appendix C

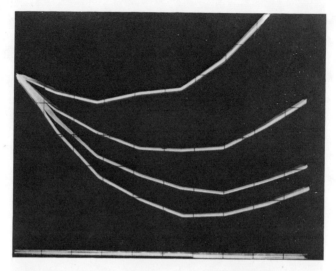

Fig. A.C.6. $\eta = \vartheta = 0$; $\lambda = 0.17$; $\mu = 0.00, 0.10, 0.18$ and 0.25.

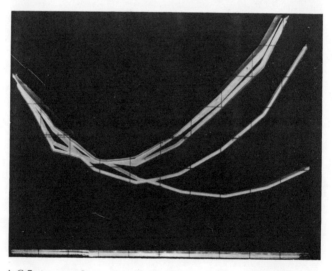

Fig. A.C.7. $\lambda = \mu = 0$; $(\eta, \vartheta) = (0.00, \ 0.00),$ $(0.25, \ 0.25),$ $(0.50, \ 0.40)$ and $(0.75, 0.75)$.

15 Fig. A.C.8 shows the sensitivity of the I^t curve to variations in both λ and μ. First, the curve moves down in the diagram. Then it moves up as the values of λ and μ increase. Especially for the end of the period considered.

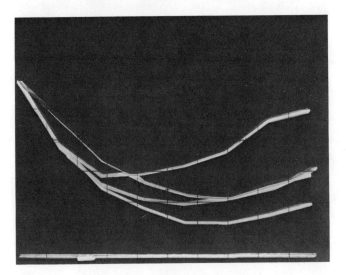

Fig. A.C.8. $\eta = \vartheta = 0$; $(\lambda, \mu) = (0.00,\ 0.00),\ (0.40,\ 0.10),\ (0.70,\ 0.25)$ and $(1.00, 0.40)$.

16 Fig. A.C.9 shows the sensitivity of the I^t curve to variations in all of the four parameters. The curve moves down to the left and up to the right as the parameter values increase.

Running a Cobb–Douglas Heckscher–Ohlin model

17 The exercise above illustrates how complicated it makes a model to allow for regional differences in technology and the growth of productivity. A conventional economist would assume such difficulties away. He would work with an ordinary Cobb–Doublas Heckscher–Ohlin model.

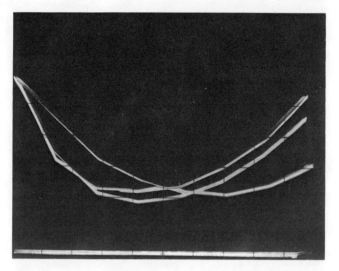

Fig. A.C.9. $(\eta, \vartheta, \lambda, \mu) = (0.00, 0.00, 0.00, 0.00)$, $(0.25, 0.25, 0.40, 0.10)$ and $(0.50, 0.35, 0.70, 0.18)$.

In such a model the regional production functions could be:

$$Y_i^t = (K_i^t)^{0.25}(L_i^t)^{0.75}. \tag{A.C.9}$$

The development over time of the regional factor endowments could be determined as follows:

$$K_i^{t+1} = K_i^t \cdot \left(\frac{r_i^t}{r^t}\right)^\eta, \tag{A.C.10}$$

$$L_i^{t+1} = L_i^t \cdot \left(\frac{w_i^t}{w^t}\right)^\lambda. \tag{A.C.11}$$

The values of the status variables could be those given by table A.C.2.

TABLE A.C.2

i	K_i^{1880}	L_i^{1880}
	Units	Units
1	9	1
2	8	2
3	7	3
4	6	4
5	5	5
6	4	6
7	3	7
8	2	8
9	1	9
Total	45	45

18 The digital component of the hybrid computer could be programmed as follows:

```
C                       MAIN PROGRAM
C
      COMMON IY,IAK,IAL,EP
      DIMENSION IAK(3,10),IAL(3,10),IY(3,10),EP(205)
      I=0
      DO 5 J=0,2040,10
      I=I+1
      RR=FLOAT(J)/100.
5     EP(I)=EXP(RR)
      EP(205)=EXP(20.50)
      DO 1 I=1,10
      READ(1,10)IY(1,I)
      READ(1,10)IAK(1,I)
1     READ(1,10)IAL(1,I)
      DO 4 I=1,10
      II=I+10
      WRITE(1,13)EP(II)
4     WRITE(1,12)IY(1,I),IAK(1,I),IAL(1,I)
      PAUSE 1
10    FORMAT(I5)
13    FORMAT(E11.5)
12    FORMAT(7X,I7,3X,I5,3X,I5,3X,I5)
      END
```

```
C                 PROCESS
C
       COMMON IY,IAK,IAL,EP
       DIMENSION Y(10),IY(3,10),IAK(3,10),IAL(3,10)
       DIMENSION RX(2),EP(205),IVK1(10),IVK3(10)
1004   MX=1
       RX(1)=1.06
       IT=0
1000   IF(IT-10)60,61,60
61     CALL DAC(6,0)
       CALL DAC(6,1060)
60     DO 40 I=1,10
       IY(2,I)=IY(MX,I)
       IAK(2,I)=IAK(MX,I)
40     IAL(2,I)=IAL(MX,I)
       RX(2)=0.
       IT=IT+10
       P5=IADC(0)
       P5=P5/2047.
       P2=IADC(2)
       P2=P2/2047.
       DO 7 I=1,10
       IL=FLOAT(IAL(2,I))*0.75
       IK=-FLOAT(IAK(2,I))*0.75
       JK=FLOAT(IAK(2,I))*0.25
       JL=-FLOAT(IAL(2,I))*0.25
       IVK1(I)=IL+IK-138
7      IVK3(I)=JK+JL-29
       A1=0.
       A2=0.
       DO 8 I=2,10
       IVK1(I)=IVK1(I)-IVK1(1)
       IVK3(I)=IVK3(I)-IVK3(1)
       IAK(3,I)=FLOAT(IAK(2,I))+FLOAT(IVK1(I))*P2
       IAL(3,I)=FLOAT(IAL(2,I))+FLOAT(IVK3(I))*P5
       A1=A1+EP(IAK(3,I)/10+1)
       IPL=IAL(3,I)/10+1
       REL=IREM(XX)
8      A2=A2+EP(IPL)+(EP(IPL+1)-EP(IPL))/10.*REL
       IAK(3,1)=ELOG(A1)*100.
       IAL(3,1)=ELOG(A2)*100.
       DO 20 I=1,10
       IK=FLOAT(IAK(3,I))*0.25
       IL=FLOAT(IAL(3,I))*0.75
       IY(3,I)=IK+IL
       IPY=IY(3,I)/10+1
       REY=IREM(XX)
20     Y(I)=EP(IPY)+(EP(IPY+1)-EP(IPY))/10.*REY
       DO 21 I=2,10
       IR=IY(3,I)+IAL(3,I)-IAL(3,1)
       IPR=IR/10+1
       RRR=IREM(XX)
       RR=EP(IPR)+(EP(IPR+1)-EP(IPR))/10.*RRR
21     RX(2)=RX(2)+(Y(I)-RR)/RR*(Y(I)-RR)/RR
       IDX=(RX(2)-RX(1))*2000.
       CALL DAC(7,IDX)
       M=RX(2)*1000.
       CALL DAC(0,M)
       MX=3
       RX(1)=RX(2)
       IF(IT-70)1000,1004,1004
       END
```

19   Fig. A.C.10 shows the I^t curve, given $\eta = \lambda = 0$. In principle, it is horizontal. The small variations are explained by "noise" in the computer system.

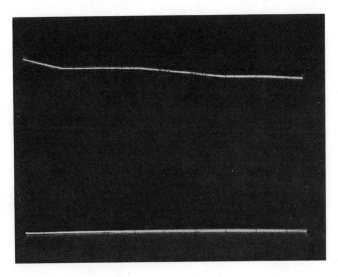

Fig. A.C.10. $\eta = \lambda = 0$.

20 Fig. A.C.11 shows how sensitive I^t is to variations in η, given $\lambda = 0$. The curve moves down in the diagram as the value of η increases.

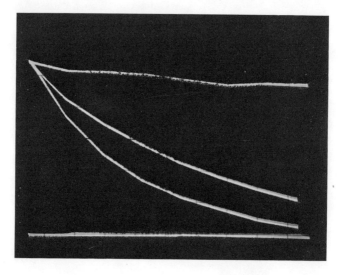

Fig. A.C.11. $\lambda = 0$; $\eta = 0.00, 0.10$ and 0.18.

21 Fig. A.C.12 shows the sensitivity of the I^t curve to variations in λ, given $\eta = 0$. The curve moves down in the diagram as the value of λ increases.

22 Fig. A.C.13 shows how sensitive I^t is to variations of both η and λ. The curve moves down in the diagram as the parameter values increase.

23 Figs. A.C.11–A.C.13 certify how well behaved the Cobb–Doublas Heckscher–Ohlin model is. Life of the conventional economist is easy. But is it worth living?

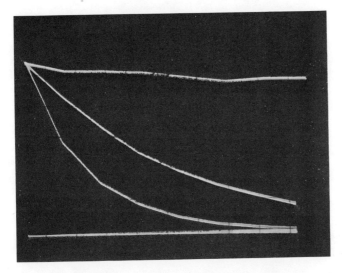

Fig. A.C.12. $\eta = 0$; $\lambda = 0.00, 0.40$ and 1.00.

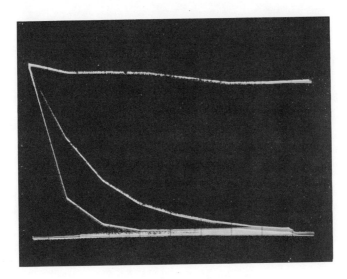

Fig. A.C.13. $(\eta, \lambda) = (0.00, 0.00), (0.20, 0.40)$ and $(0.40, 1.00)$.

The film

24 Figs. A.C.2–A.C.13 are photographs of the computer's display screen at given points of time. Readers wanting to follow the whole exercise on the display screen can buy a film which is sold as an extra to this book.

INDEX

Sammenfatning på dansk

Formålet med denne bog er at præsentere, sammenligne og samarbejde tre teorier for den internationale og interregionale handel.

I bogens første del præsenteres de tre teoribygninger: Heckscher–Ohlin skolens, den sociale fysiks og Gunnar Myrdals.

I bogens anden del samarbejdes væsentlige dele fra hver af de tre teorier i en økonomisk model i tid og sted. Modellen bestemmer de regionale indkomstforskelle.

I bogens tredje del sammenholdes modellen med den historiske udvikling i USA fra 1880 til 1950. Konklusionen er, at det ikke går helt galt.

Et appendix gennemgår en ny teknik: Sensitivitets-analyse på en hybrid computer. Man kan på en fjernsynsskærm følge virkningerne af trinløse parametervariationer. F. eks. kan man se, hvorledes det går med de regionale indkomstforskelle, når arbejdskraftens geografiske bevægelighed øges eller mindskes. En film, der kan købes sammen med bogen, viser et sådant eksempel.